GOLD FROM THE SAND

To Dad.

Happy Birthday "06"

Lots of Love

Paul & Joann

x xx.

GOLD FROM THE SAND

DAVID BELLINGHAM

Raceform

Dedication
To Clare

Many thanks to Tracey Scarlett, Fiona Pike, Julian Brown and Richard Lowther for their help in the creation of this book.

Published in 2005 by Raceform Ltd
Compton, Newbury, Berkshire, RG20 6NL
Raceform Ltd is a wholly-owned subsidiary of Trinity-Mirror plc

A catalogue record for this book is available from the British Library.

ISBN 1-905153-15-5

Cover designed by Tracey Scarlett
Interiors designed by Fiona Pike

Printed in Great Britain by William Clowes Ltd, Beccles, Suffolk

CONTENTS

INTRODUCTION

When I was asked to write the original *Gold from the Sand* in the spring of 2000, the very idea of it blew my mind. The task seemed enormous, as I had never written anything on the same scale before and I never believed that I could achieve it, but somehow I did. After the book was published in the autumn of that year, I was quite certain that was going to be about it as far as my career as an author was concerned. After all, every single one of my views and experiences with regard to All-Weather racing went into that book, so there was going to be nothing else to say. Or at least so I thought.

Real life, as I'm sure you are aware, isn't like that. The world changes, even racing occasionally changes (though there are many who wish it didn't) and there was no way I could have foreseen the changes that were soon about to occur in the relatively small world of All-Weather racing. Within a few months of the publication of the first book, which included everything you needed to know about Equitrack, Lingfield decided to do away with that surface following a series of problems, and replace it with a new high-quality and much more resilient surface.

Consequently, in the November of 2001, 13 months after the publication of the original *Gold From The Sand*, Lingfield staged the first meeting on its new Polytrack, therefore rendering a sizeable part of the first book redundant and creating a whole new headache for punters as regards how to treat the new surface. We all had to learn about the idiosyncrasies of Polytrack from scratch, and many learnt the hard way.

The wind of change didn't stop there though. Wolverhampton began to experience similar problems with its surface and so, after almost 11 years of racing on Fibresand at Dunstall Park, they too took the Polytrack route in October 2004. Two other changes to have also taken place in recent years, which are of major significance to All-Weather racing, have been the development of betting exchanges and the introduction of Regional racing (sometimes referred to as banded racing) at the start of 2004.

All of this has made it necessary to revise and update *Gold From The Sand* to reflect the racing world we now live in. No doubt there will be a need to do so again in the future, especially when the new sand tracks at

Kempton, Newbury and Great Leighs come online next year, whilst others are likely to follow soon after. For now, I will deal with the situation as it stands, i.e. the Lingfield and Wolverhampton Polytrack surfaces and the good old faithful Southwell Fibresand.

Although some things have changed within the past five years, there haven't been enough of them to justify a whole new book. Those views and opinions that I consider to be as relevant now as they were at the change of the millennium have been left unaltered, but where an update is necessary (the draw statistics being the most obvious example) the original script has been updated. This of course means that anyone who read the original book will come across some familiar passages. Apologies for that, but I did not feel it was necessary to tamper with a piece of text that is just as meaningful now as it ever was just for the sake of it.

There is a completely new diary towards the end of the book however, covering my visits to seven All-Weather meetings during the spring and summer of 2005. The meetings covered may seem rather spread out, but when I was asked to update this book in the spring of 2005, the core All-Weather season had virtually come to an end, plus the meetings that I could attend had to fit in amongst work commitments. It was very important to me to include a new diary though, in order to show that the methods I use, and have expounded in this book, continue to be successful.

In the first book, I did not dedicate any space to the relevance of breeding or whether a horse is more or less likely to take to the sand because of its pedigree. I preferred to rely on hard evidence shown on the track to formulate my opinions, in other words go by what has actually happened on the track rather than by guesswork. I still do, but do concede that it's another piece of information that might prove useful, so at the end of each chapter covering each individual track there is a list of sires whose progeny have been most successful at that venue between August 2003 and July 2005.

I have rarely backed any horse that has been making its racecourse debut on sand or in any All-Weather contest where none of the runners has raced before, but if I do then information like this is obviously going to be extremely relevant and it would be plain silly to ignore it.

One other new feature in this updated version is right at the end of the book, and is something of an opportunity for self-indulgence. I have called it the 'Roll Of Honour', which is basically a chance to salute those horses that have achieved the most success in British All-Weather Flat racing since the whole thing began in October 1989.

I feel that even now there still seems to be something of a stigma attached to All-Weather racing, though admittedly it's not quite as pronounced as it used to be, thanks to several horses coming off the sand and going on to win decent races on turf, even up to Group-race level. Even so, quite often when a horse wins a decent race on turf having previously been running on sand, some people throw their hands in the air in disbelief and exclaim 'But this horse has been running on the All-Weather!' as if the horse must have been taking several steps up in class by switching from sand to turf. That opinion may have had a grain of truth to it in the early days of the All-Weather, as the quality of the horses was not great, but that was originally the whole point of the game in the first place. It was tactfully described as being an opportunity for the smaller owners, trainers and less-glamorous jockeys to earn some cash whilst their more well-off and successful colleagues bronzed themselves on a tropical beach or enjoyed a nice little earner rushing around the racecourses of Hong Kong.

Things are a bit different now. Horses are winning races on the sand during the winter before going on to make their mark in decent contests on turf. Others are ending up racing abroad, including in the United States where the money that can be won is huge by our own modest standards. Another feature of recent seasons has been the way in which some talented young riders have emerged after riding a few winners on sand during the winter, so when you attend a meeting on a crisp, cold day in January, you may well be seeing some of the headline-makers of the future on two legs as well as four.

Ask some people which is the classier event, a Class 4 handicap on sand or a race of a similar grade on turf, and there will be many who will say the latter, but rather like the old riddle 'Which is the heavier, a ton of feathers or a ton of coal?' The answer is that there is no difference. A Class 4 handicap is a Class 4 handicap irrespective of the racing surface. However, that is not to say that the same horse is guaranteed to be able to win a race at that level on both turf and sand, and that is where most punters go wrong. The different discipline of All-Weather racing means that the form assessment required to try and predict the likely outcome of a race on sand needs to be heavily biased in favour of previous form shown on that surface. Turf form is purely incidental to the likely outcome of an All-Weather race and that message cannot be emphasised too strongly. I make no apology for repeating it throughout these pages.

The majority of races on sand are very competitive when compared with many events that take place on grass, especially when the turf gets firm. It also helps if you back a few winners, and of course hopefully this book will help in that respect. All-Weather racing is still a relatively new game to many and, as with any new game, a guide as to how to play it is a great help. That is the whole point of this book and I hope that it might just encourage one or two people to go along to an All-Weather fixture and find out what it's all about.

CHAPTER ONE

ORIGINS

The air was thick with expectation and the huge crowd looked on as the runners were led around behind the starting gate. From my position about half a furlong beyond the winning line, I had a pretty good view of the six-furlong start and I could just about see the finish, though the horses would be running more or less straight towards me down the *stretch*. The last word in that previous sentence gives a clue to where I was, as we are not talking about a cold winter's day at Wolverhampton here. The month was November and the temperature was indeed only just above freezing, but this was Breeders' Cup VIII at Churchill Downs in Louisville, Kentucky and the runners were just about to be loaded into the gates for the 1991 Breeders' Cup Sprint.

This was my first experience of racing in America, and indeed my first ever visit to the 'Land Of The Free'. Just a couple of days earlier I had been privileged to visit two major stud farms in Kentucky and see the likes of Riverman and Mr Prospector being paraded in front of me, as well as being able to see Secretariat's grave. Thanks to the wonderful organisation of Horse Racing Abroad, I was now fulfilling a lifetime's ambition by attending a race meeting the other side of the Atlantic. Not just any meeting either, but a celebration of the best horseflesh from two continents.

Although the Breeders' Cup Sprint was not the first race I had ever seen run on anything apart from grass (I had also attended Churchill Downs the previous day and one race had been run on the dirt before the BC Sprint), this event was to have a profound effect on me. This particular trip to the States had provided me with the opportunity to meet up with some American pen-friends who were also huge racing fans. As we all stood next to the parade ring, we discussed the relative merits of the runners taking part in the BC Sprint, and it soon became clear that my American friends would not hear of defeat for their favourite, a horse called Housebuster. That view also seemed to be held by most people on the track judging by his pari-mutuel (Tote) odds. Amongst all of this enthusiasm and no doubt well-intentioned patriotism (the Americans do like a winner), there was to be heard one dissenting English voice amongst the throngs, i.e. mine. I remember this voice rather feebly whispering, 'You know, I have to say that our Sheikh Albadou is a very good horse'.

Whether anyone actually heard me say that was difficult to ascertain at the time. My friends just smiled politely and you could almost tell what they were thinking, something like 'How sweet, our English visitor has just made a quaint statement bordering on the deranged. I wonder what he thinks of our country?' (All Americans seem to want to know what we think of their country). Nevertheless, I made my way, unperturbed, to place my wager on the pari-mutuel and was quite prepared to invest a not inconsiderable amount of money on Sheikh Albadou.

For anyone who has ever played Monopoly, or any other game where pretend money is involved, this will make more sense. You know how you feel when you are playing with fake money? It's not real is it? Therefore you can be quite liberal with it and you tend to throw it around in a very different way to real pounds and pence. That is how I felt about the dollar bills I was now pulling from my wallet and pushing across the counter. It was Mickey Mouse money really, and I didn't feel the same emotional constraints that I do when placing a sizeable bet at home. Had I done a quick calculation of the exchange rate in my head, I would probably have frightened myself, but I was in a holiday mood and was getting caught up in the excitement of the day.

I had been looking with great interest at the British bookmakers' prices on the Breeders' Cup races before flying out, and Sheikh Albadou had been generally quoted at about 8-1. However, at the moment I pushed my bundle of dollar bills across the counter, his odds on the pari-mutuel were a massive 25-1. This was perhaps not so surprising when you consider that no British-trained horse had ever previously won a Breeders' Cup race on dirt, and memories of Dayjur's shadow-jumping exploits the previous year were still fresh in the memory. Despite all that, I still wanted to back him at those odds and I was quite happy as I took my seat close to the rails on the Clubhouse turn.

When the stalls eventually burst open for the BC Sprint there was a huge roar from the massive Churchill Downs crowd, the sort of noise not often heard on British tracks, even for the biggest races, but in America they know how to create an atmosphere for a sporting event and they were certainly doing it here. At about the halfway stage of the contest, I could just about make out Pat Eddery's red and white colours aboard Sheikh Albadou in about fourth place, not too far off the pace and still seemingly going well. Just after that, the course commentator exclaimed that Housebuster had hit the front, which was greeted with an even louder roar from the crowd. At that stage I thought that whatever Sheikh Albadou did from then on, he'd run a blinder and certainly hadn't let anyone down, but still Pat Eddery had not yet gone for everything.

Within a couple of seconds, I was watching in almost joyous disbelief as Sheikh Albadou came flying down the outside of the track, went past Housebuster as if he were standing still, and zipped clear for a three-length victory. As he flashed past the post, there were only a few voices still roaring amongst the crowd and one of them was mine. Anyone that knows me will testify as to how reticent I am during the course of most races, but on this occasion I completely lost my head. Several 'yee-hahs' emerged from my lips as I made my way towards the back of the stands, much to the amusement of the many Americans stood around me. I soon met up with my pen-friends again and they were smiling as broadly as I was. They had remembered what I had said about Sheikh Albadou beforehand and even though none of them had invested any money on him, they were genuinely pleased for me and for the horse. Sporting generosity at its best.

As a result of that victory I picked up a very tidy sum in dollar bills, though to this day I'm still not sure exactly how much I won. All I know is that it virtually paid for the entire two-week holiday in Kentucky and New Orleans. The fun didn't end there though. I went on to back more winners in Arazi (who made such a big impression in the Breeders' Cup Juvenile) and Black Tie Affair in the BC Classic. To cap it all, two young American gentlemen who happened to work for Lipton's Tea wanted to know what I thought of their country.

Between All-Weather racing starting in this country with the victory of Niklas Angel at Lingfield in October 1989, up until my visit to America in 1991, I had only ever witnessed racing on sand via the SIS service in my local betting shop. I had placed bets on All-Weather contests many times, as I didn't really care what sort of surface the race was being run on. The main thing was that it was a horserace and therefore could not be allowed to pass by without trying to win some money on it, but that meant I was guilty of placing bets on a type of racing I didn't really know enough about. It may seem ironic now, but in those days I was rather unnerved by the prospect of All-Weather racing taking hold in this country. I didn't like the idea of our wonderful emerald-green turf tracks being dug up and converted into some sort of ugly brown building site, but in reality any anti-All-Weather bias I might have had disappeared at a stroke on that cold autumn day in 1991.

My next experience of racing on sand was when I attended the following year's Breeders' Cup at Gulfstream Park in Miami. It was always going to be difficult to repeat the previous year's successes both for myself and for the European horses that were trying to land the big bucks that year, and so it was to prove. However, there was one abiding memory from that particular meeting which has stayed with me ever since, and was to have a major impact on my thinking on the whole concept of All-Weather racing.

The field for the Breeders' Cup Classic included one of the top British-trained three-year-old colts of the 1990s in Rodrigo De Triano. The Peter Chapple-Hyam-trained colt had already won four Group One races that year, the English and Irish 2000 Guineas, the Juddmonte International and the Champion Stakes. Had the Breeders' Cup Classic been run on turf then he would surely have taken all the beating, but the Breeders' Cup Classic is run on dirt and so it was desperately sad to see this talented horse stop as if shot even before the turn out of the back stretch had been reached.

My knowledge of racing on sand was still pretty limited in those days, especially with regards to how reliable form shown on one surface was in the context of another. This race was to prove a valuable landmark in the learning process though, as it made me think about the differences between the two surfaces and how they relate to each other from the form student's point of view. These days my philosophy on such matters is pretty clear and provides one of the two major rules by which I manage to exist from one day to the next.

- Whilst out driving in your car, be very wary of any other road user who is driving whilst wearing a hat.

- Form shown on one type of racing surface is purely incidental in the likely outcome of a race on another.

The following year I returned to the Breeders' Cup once again, this time being held at Santa Anita racetrack near Los Angeles. After six of the seven races had been run, the day threatened to be another complete wipe-out for the Europeans, but then up cropped the French-trained Arcangues, who provided one of the biggest shocks in Breeders' Cup history by winning the Classic at pari-mutuel odds of 133-1. Needless to say I didn't back him, but the day was to provide another key moment in my development as an All-Weather disciple.

Andy Beyer is the guru of speed ratings on the other side of the Atlantic. In fact he is so closely identified with speed figures, that his surname is often used instead of the term 'speed figure'. People will ask which horse has the top 'Beyer', meaning which horse has the top speed figure. His ratings also made their way into the *Daily Racing Form* (America's equivalent of the *Racing Post*) and he had also previously written three very successful books on speed handicapping, as well as penning the racing column for the *Washington Post*.

As luck would have it, Andy Beyer's fourth book had just been published and he was holding a signing session here at Santa Anita. Called *Beyer On Speed*, the book was not a celebration of the joys of illegal substances, but a highly entertaining and informative piece on how to handicap races using speed figures as the basis. I could not resist buying a copy before joining the queue to get it signed by the great man. When my turn finally arrived, I felt very nervous though I'm not quite sure why. Perhaps I was aware that my English accent was very noticeable to those around me, but whatever the reason I came out with what seemed a complete load of incomprehensible claptrap about how I was keen to get back to England and use his methods on our All-Weather tracks. He smiled as we chatted, possibly thinking, 'Who is this idiot? I wonder what he thinks of our country?' Despite that, the overriding impression I got was that he thought my idea of using his methods back home was a sound one.

I then started to think very seriously about what Andy Beyer and I had discussed, plus the future direction I wanted to take with my betting. In those days speed figures were still very much a minority approach to handicapping races in Britain and, unlike in America where Andy Beyer's speed figures were driving the odds of his top-rated horses down, over here horses that had previously run fast times (allowing for the track conditions) were still starting at relatively generous prices. Also, unlike in America, we do not have a Tote monopoly over here so any advantage I could gain through taking an individual approach would be boosted by the ability to shop around for the biggest price. I decided that I would make a serious attempt to become a successful punter by concentrating on All-Weather racing only, and using speed figures as my main tool.

There were three main reasons for this:

1) It seemed to me that speed figures would work best when used to evaluate truly run races, and All-Weather races are run at a truer pace than the majority of those run on turf.

2) By specialising in racing on sand I was effectively making the whole sport a bit more compact and therefore the number of horses I would be dealing with was going to be much more manageable, as opposed to trying to keep tabs on every single horse in training. After a while, I would get to know most of the horses well and would have a better chance of getting to know their requirements, and their quirks if any.

3) I was quite happy to ignore form shown on grass and concentrate on a horse's previous performances on sand as my main guide. Doing this would also very likely put me at odds with most other punters, but that was no bad thing when those same punters are the ones who will decide the shape of the betting market on a particular race.

That is not to say I was going to stop going to turf meetings completely. This was a decision based purely on the betting angle and from now on my largest investments were going to be on All-Weather races. That was going to become my area of expertise, but as someone who was brought up watching the likes of Nijinsky, Mill Reef, Brigadier

Gerard and Red Rum race in the flesh, attending turf meetings on the Flat and over jumps was still going to be an important part of my life.

My first visit to a British All-Weather meeting was to come just two months after getting back from the 1993 Breeders' Cup, and partly by accident.

In those days, before I was married, my mother and I often went away on short racing breaks, usually some distance away from home, and would therefore make a small holiday of it. In January 1994, we had planned to do one of these trips. The original idea was to drive up to the midlands on the Thursday, go racing at Towcester on the Friday, and then drive down to Sandown for the Mildmay-Cazalet meeting on the Saturday. Unfortunately, the weather took a turn for the worse with the arrival of snow and meetings started to be abandoned. Towcester looked very doubtful for the Friday and so we decided that rather than miss out, we would make our way up to Southwell on the Friday if Towcester were abandoned.

Just in case that was to happen, I spent the whole of Thursday evening in my hotel room with a calculator, pen and paper, putting together some speed ratings for the Southwell card.

The following morning, Towcester was indeed abandoned and so we made our way through a very snowy scene up to Nottinghamshire to hopefully end up at Southwell racecourse, though it did become a rather slow and complex journey before we eventually made it.

I remember being quite surprised when finally reaching the course. I wasn't exactly sure what to expect, but what I found was a comfortable, friendly racetrack with modern facilities, even if the stands were not exactly bursting at the seams. Anyway, the important thing was that I was keen to see how well my hastily calculated speed figures were going to work in the heat of battle. I consulted my wrinkled piece of A4 to try and predict the winner of the first race, a seven-furlong all-age maiden. In those days, all winners from 1 January counted towards the Jockeys' Championship, so both Frankie Dettori and Jason Weaver were there and indeed it was Frankie who was aboard my top-rated horse, the Lord Huntingdon-trained Akabusi. The trainer was also at the track, which for some reason rather surprised me at the time. Perhaps I had become so used to seeing him in the paddock on a hot day at a crowded Ascot, that it seemed a bit strange to see him on a freezing cold afternoon at Southwell.

Nonetheless, with the feeling that I was starting out on an exciting new venture, I made my way to the betting ring to place my bet on Akabusi. There was some 9/4 available, which seemed quite reasonable to me considering how much he had in hand according to my speed ratings. I placed my investment and made my way up to the stands to watch the race.

Once under way, the contest seemed to go exactly the way I thought it would. That may seem a bit of an arrogant statement, but the speed figures in my possession not only gave me an insight into which horse was likely to win, they also told me how much one horse was faster than another and the likely result if all the runners performed somewhere near their best. As we all know, horses do not always run as fast as they can, which helps provide the uncertainty that shapes the betting market.

A good comparison is athletics. Time is very much used as the barometer by which athletes on the track are measured and, more often than not, they run true to form and the fastest man or woman usually wins. If there were the same amount of betting opportunities on athletics as there are on horses, then there would be quite a few very short-priced favourites. Fortunately for us, not many horses start at the sort of odds the fastest athletes would, but standouts do exist from time to time. It's just a question of spotting them. In reality, the four-legged version of Akabusi was exactly that type of standout, but I was still new to the game and did not invest the sort of sums that I would these days.

Akabusi made the running and never really looked like being caught. I remember thinking at the time that although it was a good start for me, it was only one race. At least I had done my homework and this was not just a case of sticking a pin in the newspaper and hoping for the best. I also knew that there were another six races still to go, and the card as a whole would provide a better indicator as to how I was going to get on at this game.

As it turned out, the meeting was to prove a key moment in my burgeoning enthusiasm for All-Weather racing. Of the seven races run the day, I had straight win bets in five of them and all five won. Apart from Akabusi winning at 2/1, Just Harry (11/8), No Submission (3/1), Warwick Warrior (3/1) and Royal Citizen (7/1) all contributed to an unforgettable day. There was even a point when I felt a little sorry for the on-course bookmakers, as with the horses seemingly running to form it appeared they had no chance. I quickly recovered from that little faux pas, but even these days I do not view bookmakers as 'the enemy' in quite the same way that many other people seem to. If there is an 'enemy' then it is everyone else who takes a different view to me in a particular race. The bookmakers are just the purse-holders.

I had gone to Southwell on that day with about £60 in betting money (pretty average for me in those days when I was a poor civil servant), but had emerged with over £750. Days like that, when you feel you can do little wrong, occur infrequently when you are just an enthusiastic amateur, but it convinced me that this particular type of racing was well worth persevering with and it was also extremely enjoyable. I also knew that, despite the success of that first day, I was going to have to develop a more professional approach to form study. I could only achieve this by doing my homework properly and by developing my own speed figures and my own statistics. No more hastily scribbled speed ratings in hotel rooms.

I ought to mention that in those days All-Weather jumping was still taking place, though it had not really caught my imagination in the same way that Flat racing on sand had done. That was probably just as well, because a few months later All-Weather jumping was scrapped following some ugly falls and the disastrous consequences that often occurred as a result. There have been some whispers about bringing it back in recent years, but my memories of it, quite apart from the dangers involved, are of small fields and uncompetitive racing. If they were to bring it back, I would look at it as another possible area to exploit with the aid of speed figures, statistics and the like, but I rather hope they don't.

Having read many books on horse-race betting, most of them written by American authors such as Andy Beyer, I came to the conclusion that if I were to get anywhere in this game then I was going to have to specialise in All-Weather racing in every sense of the word. I was going to have to know more about the horses that ran on the surface than the vast majority of the punters I was betting against. Basically, I was going to have to become the equivalent of someone sat at a poker game who was able to observe the hands held by everyone else. As I stated before, I would only give a very small amount of attention to previous form shown on turf when assessing a race on sand and I knew that wouldn't be so with most other people. As far as I was concerned, the only significance of a race on turf, when analysing a race on sand, is that it might help to confirm a horse's fitness, but the actual performance of the horse in the race itself would be of limited significance.

One more memorable event was to take place just before I finally took the plunge and bought a computer on which to calculate my speed ratings and draw statistics. Having just returned from attending the three-day York Ebor meeting in August 1995, myself and my family decided to make our first visit to a Wolverhampton Saturday evening meeting and sample the delights of the Zongalero Restaurant (more details in Chapter Four). I know I previously said that hastily putting together speed figures was going to be a thing of the past, but I was going to have to do just that for this meeting because of the limited amount of time available to me, so I spent most of the Friday evening with a pen, a piece of paper, a form book and a calculator.

Come the following evening, armed with my speed figures and a bit of knowledge on the effects of the draw, I spent a very enjoyable few hours observing some competitive racing from the comfort of Wolverhampton's Zongalero restaurant, whilst also enjoying a fine, warm summer's evening. Two memorable moments stand out from that meeting at Dunstall Park. Firstly, whilst waiting to place a bet on the first race, I noticed a fairly short man with long hair, beard and rose-coloured glasses standing in the Tote queue ahead of me. It was only when he turned around that I realised who he was. It was none other than Roy Wood! For those of you who were born after the Cuban Missile Crisis, Roy Wood was a very big name in popular music throughout the late Sixties and early Seventies, having been vocalist with bands such as The Move and Wizzard. His dulcet tones can still be heard to this day in fact, most noticeably at Christmas when they churn out 'I Wish It Could Be Christmas Every Day' almost everywhere you go.

As far as the racing was concerned, my speed figures once again unearthed an absolute peach. In the six-furlong handicap, it seemed pretty obvious to me that Four Of Spades had a major chance and I placed a £20 win bet on the Tote (this was a social evening more than anything else and, as it's a very long way from the restaurant to the betting ring, all of my bets on this particular evening were on the 'nanny').

After the stalls opened, the field sped down the back straight, kicking up a trail of sand which became illuminated by the setting sun. At that stage, Four Of Spades was racing well off the pace, but once into the home straight he came with a strong run down the outside under Amanda Sanders and got up to win in the dying strides. I hadn't taken much notice of the Tote screens before the race, but I certainly did now! For my £20 outlay, I was picking up well over £400, which was particularly rewarding as in reality I had not gone to the meeting with any great ambitions.

A couple of months later my new computer arrived. I soon began to create a purely All-Weather database, which I nicknamed 'Adonis' (the top speed figures earned under this system are shown at the end of the book) and which I have been maintaining at home ever since. Following plenty of toil and sweat, mostly involving going back through some dusty old *Raceform* annuals, I have now achieved my goal of holding every single performance of every horse that has ever run in an All-Weather Flat race in Britain. All of it was entered manually, hence the sore fingers, but it has been crucial in enabling me to untangle the labyrinthine form lines that exist within All-Weather racing, and adopt a strategy that is explained in more detail later in the book.

There was definitely an anti-All-Weather bias in the early years after its introduction in 1989, but I do think that attitudes have changed a lot since then even if some prejudice remains. The sport of horse racing is, by its very nature, still very conservative and it takes time for new innovations to be accepted. No-one wants to see sand replacing turf as the traditional surface on which British racing is held, least of all me, but All-Weather racing has its place within the structure of the sport in this country, especially during the winter months when it holds centre stage if National Hunt meetings fall to the elements. There is no arguing with the fact that, especially in those early years, the general quality of horses racing on sand was pretty moderate, partly because of the way races were framed in catering for those at the lower end of the scale. Even the jockeys who rode right through the winter were grouped in the same category.

These days it's still very much the exception rather than the rule to see a Class 3 race or better run at an All-Weather meeting, but the exploits of the globetrotting Running Stag in the late 90s as well as other successful exports to the US did much to raise the profile of the game. It also seemed as though some members of the media had double standards in their views on racing on artificial surfaces. The Dubai World Cup has been won by some of the world's very best thoroughbreds, such as Dubai Millennium, and I don't remember anyone referring to him as an All-Weather horse, but that is surely what he was on the day.

The quality of horses that race on sand has definitely gone up in recent years and one major reason for that is the near-universal praise that has been heaped on the Polytrack surface by trainers and jockeys alike. Trainers are quite happy to allow their better horses to race on that surface now and some top stables run their decent younger horses in Polytrack maidens knowing they are racing on a kind, consistent surface. These days few people are surprised when a horse comes off the Polytrack and wins a high-class race on turf. Even some Group-race winners started their careers off on sand, but that would have been almost unthinkable over ten years ago.

Another major factor in raising the profile of sand racing has been improvements in prize money. On most Saturdays throughout the winter, the afternoon All-Weather card will feature at least one race worth upwards of £20,000. Even some midweek meetings feature a decent prize and Arena Leisure should be applauded for it. When the new All-Weather tracks start up next year, the opportunities for sand horses can only become greater.

A few years ago, the people in charge of All-Weather racing were obviously becoming sensitive to the stigma of the term 'All-Weather' and Lingfield ran a competition for people to come up with a new name for sand racing. I've never been a great fan of the term 'All-Weather' to describe racing on sand, for two main reasons. Firstly, because the name suggested that sand racing was immune to the forces of nature, which meant the tracks themselves were on a hiding to nothing. Therefore if a sand meeting were abandoned due to extreme weather, there would be some people who couldn't resist a chuckle over the irony of it all. Secondly, because the name was being used to describe horses of moderate ability. As I said earlier, this goes back to the early days when All-Weather racing was originally created in order to provide opportunities for the lesser horse, trainer and jockey.

I was attending a meeting at Lingfield in the depths of winter a few years back and considerable snow had fallen in the previous 24 hours.

Getting to the track had not been easy, but we just about made it and once we were there, found ourselves part of a very small crowd indeed. In fact there was so much snow that the only part of the scenery that wasn't white was the ten-furlong brown ribbon of the old Equitrack surface. Even during the day, the maximum temperature was still below freezing and Lingfield obviously concluded that only people who really liked the place would be dedicated (or barmy) enough to attend in such conditions.

Therefore we could presumably prove to be a useful advertising tool, so a man with a shoulder-held camera was roaming the enclosures interviewing each racegoer in turn. When he eventually caught up with me, he said 'OK, now direct your answers at my finger' which he then proceeded to stick into the air about a foot to the left of his head (it gave the impression there was someone else stood there asking the questions). He then asked 'What is it that has brought you to Lingfield today?' I resisted the obvious answer of 'my car' and said something about enjoying All-Weather racing, and that the facilities were good, and that the staff were friendly, which was all very true. I'm just glad I never saw the piece of film with my interview on it as Oscar-winning material it was not!

This was the first time I had held a conversation with someone's finger since I was six months old and I found the whole experience a little weird. We were obviously something of a novelty on that day, but was I really mad? Was it an eccentric thing to do to travel 70 miles in a scene reminiscent of a Christmas card to attend an All-Weather meeting? I didn't think so. It just shows how much I enjoy the sport and the sacrifices I'm willing to make in order to enjoy it at first hand.

Another major development in my life came in 1997 when I joined *Raceform*. Before that happened, my handicapping strategy and my approach to betting only had consequences for me, but now that tipping has become a part of my job, my selections come under much greater public scrutiny.

My first chance to tip horses in public came back in 1998 when I was given the opportunity to write 'Punters' Guides' for All-Weather meetings in the now sadly defunct *Raceform On Saturday*. I enjoyed doing them right from the start, but when I drew my first blank (tipped no winners) at a meeting in October of that year, I was gutted. I didn't like it at all and felt I had let the readers down. I remember discussing how I had felt with some highly experienced and respected racing journalists and they told me I should not worry about it. It happens to everyone and you get used to it.

In the winter of 1998/99 I started writing a column in the *Racing & Football Outlook* called 'King Of The Sand'. This gave me much greater scope to publicise my theories and opinions, as well as providing selections for every All-Weather meeting between Tuesday and Sunday of each week. Best of all though, was the thrill of being responsible for a dedicated All-Weather column, as it was something I had dreamt of doing for a long time.

At the beginning of 2000 I started writing another column for *Raceform On Saturday* called 'Quicksand'. This was a 'rejects' column, or for those of you familiar with 'The Morning Line' on Channel 4, similar to Barry Dennis's 'Bismarck', except it was only for horses running on sand. The idea was to find a fancied horse that for one reason or other I didn't think would win. This is rather more difficult than it sounds and certainly a bigger task than tipping winners. Part of the problem was trying to guess which horses would head the betting market the day before the event. As it turned out, the experience of writing this column gave me an even greater insight into All-Weather racing as a whole, as it concentrated my mind more on how a race was likely to be run, and on many occasions this would provide the reason why I felt a fancied horse was likely to be beaten.

In the autumn of 2000, I was asked to take over compiling the 'Split Second' speed ratings for *Raceform* and the methods I use for that are the same as for the speed figures that are shown in this book.

Finally, and to bring the story full circle, in 2004 I attended the Breeders' Cup, at Lone Star Park in Texas, for the first time in 11 years. Ouija Board's victory in the BC Filly & Mare Turf was obviously very exciting, but it was the thrill of winning decent money on Speightstown in the BC Sprint, and especially on Ghostzapper's brilliant victory in the Classic, that brought back cherished memories of 1991.

CHAPTER TWO

LINGFIELD

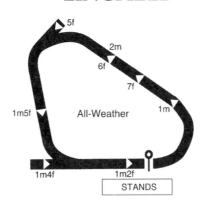

Address: Lingfield Park Racecourse, Surrey FH7 6PQ
Going & Doubtful weather: 01342 834800 or 01342 831720

Location: Lingfield Park Racecourse is located close to East Grinstead on the borders of Surrey, Kent and Sussex. Easy to get to, London is an hour away and Gatwick Airport is only 20 minutes away.

How to get there: **Road**: Follow signs to Lingfield Park from the M25 at junction 6 and pick up the A22 southbound towards East Grinstead and Eastbourne. Follow the A22 for about 4 miles to Blindley Heath. At the traffic lights take a sharp left onto the B2029 towards Lingfield. Carry on for about 2 miles, through the village. The Racecourse is at the bottom of the hill.

Rail: London Victoria Station to Lingfield Station. The Racecourse is a 5 minute walk from the adjoining station.

Air: Helicopters are permitted to land at Lingfield. Please ring the Clerk of the course on 01342 834800 to arrange landing.

Clerk of the Course: Neil MacKenzie Ross

Of the three current All-Weather tracks, Lingfield has up until now been the one I have visited the most. The facilities there are perfectly acceptable in my opinion and the renovation work on the main grandstand that took place in 2003/4 has made a big difference. A visit to the Trackside Carvery is strongly recommended if you want a combination of good food and a good view of the course, and are happy to stay in one place for the entire meeting.

The viewing for the everyday punter is fine and the great thing about All-Weather meetings during the winter is that you will have little difficulty gaining access to all the facilities, as the crowds are never that big. This is in stark contrast to some of the turf meetings they have here, especially on Saturday evenings in summer where the size of the crowd can make things a little bit tight. Unlike at Southwell and Wolverhampton, the enclosures at Lingfield comprise a lot of scattered buildings rather than one dominant structure, but this isn't a problem if you don't mind venturing outside and sampling some bracing winter air.

Thanks to the M25, the journey to Lingfield from most parts of the country is a great deal easier than it used to be. I can remember many years ago the journey taking three days across country (or at least it seemed like it), but thankfully it doesn't take quite as long as that now. Having said that, any problems on the motorway can drastically increase the journey time, especially if you get caught in the rush-hour traffic between junctions 10 and 16 on the way home!

The All-Weather track runs inside the turf and jumps courses and is left-handed and triangular-shaped, measuring just under ten furlongs round. The run-in from the final bend is about a furlong and a half, with both five-furlong and one-mile four-furlong races starting from a chute. Lingfield is undoubtedly the fastest of the three current All-Weather tracks, but despite that many horses who prefer a bit of give in the ground on turf have taken to it, and better-class animals off the grass appear to find it easier to transfer their ability onto this surface than the other two venues.

In November 2001, Lingfield replaced the old Equitrack surface with Polytrack and the general response was that the new surface was excellent. Certainly it led to trainers being more than happy to run their better horses on it and the quality of the racing has improved dramatically as a result. Lingfield had staged the Listed Winter Derby since 1998, but after the Polytrack was laid a few more races of that type were added to the programme and even Aidan O'Brien sent a horse called Castle Gandolfo over to win a Listed contest in April 2002.

Then in 2003, my prayers were finally answered when a two-day mini All-Weather Festival replaced the one-day mixed National Hunt/All-

Weather Winter Derby Meeting. The second day includes two Listed events, one being the Winter Derby itself, together with some valuable supporting contests and even the first two-year-old race of the year. The fixture has also become a fitting climax to the winter season and the contrast with how things were ten years ago couldn't be greater.

Whilst I am thrilled to bits with how things improved for the introduction of Polytrack, it didn't make things any easier for the punter. In an ideal world it's best not to risk money on a new track until the surface has been established and enough data exists to make accurate deductions on the effect of the draw, the suitability or otherwise to front-runners, or the existence of any track bias. This is very much worth bearing in mind with three new All-Weather tracks on the horizon. These venues will be staging races for decades to come, so there's plenty of time to work them out and there's surely enough racing elsewhere to keep punters occupied.

While the new surface posed plenty of questions for punters, it set a real poser for the jockeys too and their response to it was interesting. The first problem was that it appeared to be almost impossible to win from the front in races of at least a mile. Jockeys almost seemed to become paranoid about being left in front in contests over the longer trips and as a result many such races were run at an absurdly slow early pace before a mad dash down the home straight.

It's hard to say just exactly when jockeys realised that they could win from the front beyond sprint trips, but even though a few horses had managed to do so before, I would still nominate Neil Callan's winning ride aboard Movie King and Darryll Holland's two victories aboard King's Thought during February/March 2003 as turning points, mainly because all three victories were achieved within a relatively short space of time. In both cases the riders involved set a decent gallop, but also judged the pace just right, which I feel is the key to winning from the front. In other words, in strongly run races you need to race prominently, whilst in slowly run races it pays to come from off the pace. This is totally at odds with racing on turf, but then again the differences between the two surfaces form the very basis of this book.

The following pages show a series of statistics for Lingfield. They cover jockeys, trainers and favourites, followed by draw and front-runners.

JOCKEYS (1 January 2002 to 31 May 2005)			
	Total W-R	Per Cent	£1 Level Stake
E Ahern	97-629	15.0	**+10.02**
D Holland	66-342	19.0	**+38.27**
Martin Dwyer	62-569	11.0	−157.05
Dane O'Neill	57-617	9.0	−186.76
N Callan	56-489	11.0	**+37.45**
I Mongan	55-637	9.0	−168.80
K Fallon	51-270	19.0	−58.39
J Quinn	46-648	7.0	−190.81
S Whitworth	44-533	8.0	−48.97
T Quinn	44-328	13.0	−34.38
S Drowne	39-502	8.0	−193.33
J-P Guillambert	39-283	14.0	−48.26
S W Kelly	35-331	11.0	−92.25
J P Spencer	33-164	20.0	**+5.55**
C Catlin	32-581	6.0	−245.53
J F Egan	31-322	10.0	−9.48
R L Moore	31-239	13.0	**+51.18**
J Fanning	30-244	12.0	**+15.76**
G Baker	29-264	11.0	**+63.75**
J Fortune	28-277	10.0	−121.50
R Hughes	28-224	13.0	−55.13
L Dettori	27-94	29.0	**+22.56**
D Sweeney	26-325	8.0	−89.67
S Sanders	23-219	11.0	−55.92
S Carson	23-254	9.0	**+34.00**
A Culhane	20-198	10.0	−61.52
F Norton	20-220	9.0	−65.25
R Winston	20-171	12.0	−7.75
P Doe	17-315	5.0	−110.30
M Fenton	19-291	7.0	−87.34
N Pollard	19-219	9.0	−61.92
N Chalmers	17-241	7.0	−89.90
M Hills	15-109	14.0	−33.76
D Corby	15-141	11.0	**+46.00**
Lisa Jones	14-267	5.0	−176.90
Pat Eddery	13-77	17.0	**+1.76**
R Miles	13-118	11.0	−21.42
J Mackay	13-175	7.0	−62.80
R Mullen	12-115	10.0	−49.02
L P Keniry	12-238	5.0	−123.25
G Carter	11-118	9.0	−62.78
Darren Williams	11-157	7.0	−87.75
Paul Eddery	10-109	9.0	**+0.75**
B Doyle	10-67	15.0	**+5.56**
S Hitchcott	10-108	9.0	−2.75
A Quinn	10-139	7.0	−80.00
O Urbina	9-133	7.0	−75.00
R Thomas	9-132	7.0	**+0.25**
T P Queally	9-151	6.0	−70.00
J F McDonald	9-211	4.0	−88.25
P Robinson	8-63	13.0	−8.68

TRAINERS

	Total W-R	2yo Stks	3yo Stks	Other Stks	2yo H'caps	3yo H'caps	Other H'caps	App'ce	A'teurs	Per cent	£1 Level stake
G L Moore	62-479	1-17	3-34	29-173	0-0	4-26	20-184	1-25	4-20	12.9	-7.35
G A Butler	54-295	11-69	7-28	14-69	0-7	7-33	12-82	3-6	0-1	18.3	+23.87
Andrew Reid	42-340	2-18	5-31	20-127	0-7	3-30	12-118	0-7	0-2	12.4	+42.56
N P Littmoden	42-449	2-23	3-62	10-124	0-10	4-43	20-160	0-15	3-12	9.4	-125.02
J Noseda	32-124	5-19	7-31	9-32	0-2	6-16	5-24	0-0	0-0	25.8	+16.68
J R Best	32-269	4-21	1-18	6-63	3-22	8-52	8-66	0-16	2-11	11.9	+5.83
B J Meehan	29-196	10-53	6-39	5-26	2-13	5-34	1-27	0-3	0-1	14.8	+15.35
C E Brittain	27-188	1-12	9-31	6-37	1-4	5-24	5-75	0-4	0-1	14.4	-16.09
A M Balding	26-238	1-32	6-35	7-70	0-3	4-27	7-64	1-4	0-3	10.9	-53.68
R Hannon	25-274	9-72	6-39	6-69	1-19	0-32	3-42	0-1	0-0	9.1	-114.99
T G Mills	25-134	7-21	7-29	4-29	0-1	2-24	4-24	1-6	0-0	18.7	-15.34
Sir Mark Prescott	24-98	2-39	1-9	5-16	4-5	7-17	5-8	0-3	0-1	24.5	-22.42
S Dow	23-339	2-11	1-25	9-125	0-1	2-24	6-130	2-16	1-7	6.8	-179.63
P Mitchell	23-218	1-7	1-18	9-80	0-4	0-16	10-77	0-12	1-4	10.1	-71.96
Miss G Kelleway	22-158	0-2	0-6	9-69	0-0	0-7	12-69	1-3	0-2	13.9	+7.83
B G Powell	22-197	0-4	0-10	12-96	0-1	0-3	10-72	0-5	0-6	11.2	-14.00
Mrs A J Perrett	21-130	7-33	3-15	5-39	0-3	2-7	4-27	0-3	0-3	16.2	-9.98
Jamie Poulton	20-239	2-8	1-14	10-99	1-5	0-14	6-80	0-13	0-6	8.4	+21.00
D R Loder	20-93	2-13	6-20	8-21	0-1	2-23	2-15	0-0	0-0	21.5	-19.33
M R Channon	19-178	1-28	6-40	5-31	1-8	0-24	5-37	1-10	0-0	10.7	-36.13
A P Jarvis	18-145	1-9	4-30	4-29	0-2	2-27	7-41	0-5	0-2	12.4	+52.50
P Howling	18-170	0-2	4-11	6-96	1-2	1-4	5-46	1-6	0-3	10.6	+7.32
D R C Elsworth	18-147	4-18	4-35	5-42	0-4	3-8	1-34	1-3	0-3	12.2	-15.26
M A Jarvis	18-79	6-21	6-16	3-18	0-4	0-8	3-11	0-1	0-0	22.8	+58.91
C A Cyzer	18-160	1-8	5-28	5-53	0-2	1-16	6-47	0-5	0-1	11.3	+11.18
K R Burke	18-207	0-8	1-14	9-74	0-2	1-20	6-76	1-10	0-3	8.7	-71.79
Miss B Sanders	17-183	1-4	0-1	6-41	1-2	0-1	9-113	0-15	0-6	9.3	-45.00
J A Osborne	17-180	3-39	4-43	2-39	1-12	3-18	3-27	1-1	0-1	9.4	-21.82
D K Ivory	17-234	0-28	4-31	8-77	0-1	4-16	0-71	1-7	0-3	7.3	-36.97
P D Evans	16-267	1-24	1-35	5-81	0-4	0-14	8-95	1-8	0-6	6.0	-159.13
C F Wall	15-97	1-11	3-16	2-28	0-0	3-11	5-27	1-2	0-2	15.5	-21.65
J W Hills	15-178	4-41	1-26	4-38	0-5	2-27	3-35	1-5	0-1	8.4	-23.50
B W Hills	15-111	4-24	5-27	5-39	1-2	0-12	0-5	0-2	0-0	13.5	-46.02

FAVOURITES			
	W-R	Per cent	£1 Level stake
2yo Stks	71-194	36.6	−0.79
3yo Stks	70-200	35.0	−27.02
3yo+ Stks	178-620	28.7	−67.48
Totals	319-1014	31.5	−95.29
2yo H'caps	13-34	38.2	**+7.58**
3yo H'caps	47-174	27.0	−15.18
3yo+ H'caps	156-653	23.9	−29.33
Totals	216-861	25.1	−36.93
App'ce	11-63	17.5	−20.50
Amateurs	9-38	23.7	−2.10
Totals	20-101	19.8	−22.60
All Favs	555-1976	28.1	−154.82

Explanation of Draw and Front-Runner Statistics

The next few pages show draw and front-runner statistics for each distance on the Lingfield Polytrack covering the two-year period from August 1st 2003 to July 31st 2005.

The draw statistics are divided into two sections. The first section separates the draw into three groups, i.e. Low, Middle and High. For the purposes of calculation, the stall numbers for each race analysed are divided into these three groups depending on the number of runners in the race. For example, in a nine-runner race, stalls 1, 2 and 3 would fall into the 'Low' category, stalls 4, 5 and 6 into the 'Middle' category, and stalls 7, 8 and 9 into the 'High' category. In a 15-runner race, stalls 1, 2, 3, 4 and 5 would fall into the 'Low' category and so on. The percentage shown next to the number of winners in each category is the overall success rate of that category in all races, i.e. 50% for the 'Low' category would mean that half of all races run over the distance in question have been won by horses drawn in the lowest third of the field.

The second section shows the record of individual stalls for each distance. The percentage shown here is the number of winners against the number of starters from that stall, i.e. 10% would mean that one in ten horses starting from that stall have won.

Beneath the draw statistics are two lines showing the record of horses that have taken an early lead in all races over that trip. The top line shows the Impact Value. Simply put, this figure shows how successful front-runners have been in winning races over the distance against the total number of horses that have tried it. An IV of 2.0 would mean that front-runners have been twice as successful over this distance than they are entitled to be, whilst an IV of 0.5 would mean they have been half as successful. The bottom line shows how many races over the trip were won by horses that led early on during the race.

The statistics for Southwell and Wolverhampton are contained in the individual chapters on each track.

The first thing that's noticeable about the draw statistics is how different things are now compared to the Equitrack. The stats for five furlongs are a good example.

On the old surface, stall one had a great record whilst winning from stall ten was basically impossible. How different things are now. Stall one has become the proverbial coffin box and how ironic it was that a horse called Treasure Cay managed to win from that stall in February 2005, because no horse had managed to do that since he himself achieved the same feat some 14 months earlier. On the other hand, stall ten now has one of the best records over the trip.

It's still best to be drawn low over six furlongs due to the proximity of the start to a long sweeping left-hand bend, but the statistics tend to even out beyond that, including over the ten-furlong trip which used to boast one of the most pronounced draw biases on the old surface. In those days you just had to be drawn low over that distance, but that's not so true now.

Admittedly, in the early days of Polytrack the ten-furlong statistics may have been rendered meaningless because many races run over the trip were a tactical mess, but that's not really the case any more and you can win from a wider range of draws these days, though you still don't want to be drawn on the extreme outside.

Things have changed a bit for front-runners too. Although they are still favoured over five furlongs to the same degree that they always were, from six furlongs to one mile their advantage is not quite as pronounced as it was, though still high enough to be a factor. On the other hand, on Equitrack front-runners had an IV of around 1.6 over ten and 12 furlongs, but that advantage has been totally eradicated on Polytrack. It is possible to win from the front over these trips, as I mentioned before, but it's still tough for front-runners over the longer distances and it's no accident that the IV for front-runners decreases in a neat downward curve as the race distance increases.

Even though the number of races run over 13 furlongs and two miles

LINGFIELD DRAW AND FRONT-RUNNER STATISTICS
1 August 2003 to 31 July 2005

5 furlongs

Draw Pos	Winners	%
Low	22	25
Middle	37	43
High	28	32

Draw No	Runners	Winners	%
1	80	4	5
2	85	12	14
3	81	10	12
4	83	12	14
5	80	14	18
6	79	9	11
7	78	9	12
8	74	6	8
9	68	2	3
10	58	9	16

Front Runners Impact Value = 2.2
26 winners from 87 races (30%)

6 furlongs

Draw Pos	Winners	%
Low	49	28
Middle	83	47
High	43	25

Draw No	Runners	Winners	%
1	166	22	13
2	172	17	10
3	164	9	5
4	170	24	14
5	167	10	6
6	162	26	16
7	162	15	9
8	164	14	9
9	153	9	6
10	140	12	9
11	124	4	3
12	105	8	8
13	43	3	7
14	34	2	6

Front Runners Impact Value = 1.7
30 winners from 175 races (17%)

7 furlongs

Draw Pos	Winners	%
Low	67	30
Middle	87	38
High	72	32

Draw No	Runners	Winners	%
1	217	17	8
2	218	21	10
3	222	13	6
4	212	17	8
5	218	29	13
6	216	19	9
7	214	14	7
8	208	18	9
9	197	11	6
10	192	19	10
11	177	11	6
12	168	10	6
13	146	15	10
14	134	7	5
15	62	4	6
16	51	1	2

Front Runners Impact Value = 1.7
33 winners from 226 races (15%)

1 mile

Draw Pos	Winners	%
Low	70	32
Middle	82	37
High	67	31

Draw No	Runners	Winners	%
1	217	17	8
2	172	17	10
3	164	9	5
4	170	24	14
5	167	10	6
6	162	26	16
7	162	15	9
8	164	14	9
9	153	9	6
10	140	12	9
11	124	4	3
12	105	8	8
13	43	3	7
14	34	2	6

Front Runners Impact Value = 1.1
27 winners from 219 races (12%)

1 mile 2 furlongs

Draw Pos	Winners	%
Low	73	33
Middle	91	41
High	58	26

Draw No	Runners	Winners	%
1	210	18	9
2	209	28	13
3	214	20	9
4	215	19	9
5	212	18	8
6	211	30	14
7	207	12	6
8	202	18	9
9	184	20	11
10	179	12	7
11	163	10	6
12	151	7	5
13	136	6	4
14	123	4	3

Front Runners Impact Value = 1.0
20 winners from 222 races (9%)

1 mile 4 furlongs

Draw Pos	Winners	%
Low	30	29
Middle	44	43
High	29	28

Draw No	Runners	Winners	%
1	101	4	4
2	98	12	12
3	99	6	6
4	99	18	18
5	100	6	6
6	96	13	14
7	95	4	4
8	93	6	6
9	85	8	9
10	82	8	10
11	67	2	3
12	58	7	12
13	51	2	4
14	46	4	9
15	39	3	8
16	31	0	0

Front Runners Impact Value = 0.7
7 winners from 103 races (7%)

1 mile 5 furlongs

Draw Pos	Winners	%
Low	7	19
Middle	13	36
High	16	44

Draw No	Runners	Winners	%
1	33	3	9
2	34	3	9
3	33	1	3
4	36	3	8
5	36	3	8
6	36	4	11
7	36	3	8
8	31	2	6
9	31	2	6
10	27	5	19
11	26	2	8
12	24	4	17
13	20	0	0
14	18	1	6

Front Runners Impact Value = 0.3
1 winner from 36 races (3%)

2 miles

Draw Pos	Winners	%
Low	3	10
Middle	16	55
High	10	34

Draw No	Runners	Winners	%
1	28	1	4
2	27	1	4
3	29	1	3
4	26	3	12
5	29	5	17
6	28	1	4
7	27	3	11
8	25	5	20
9	25	3	12
10	21	0	0
11	19	3	16
12	19	2	11
13	16	1	6
14	13	0	0

Front Runners Impact Value = 0.4
1 winner from 29 races (3%)

is relatively small, I would still be very wary of backing a front-runner over either trip, irrespective of who's aboard.

To end this chapter, on the next page is a list of the leading sires on the Lingfield Polytrack between August 2003 and July 2005.

SIRES WHOSE PROGENY HAVE WON MORE THAN SIX RACES ON THE LINGFIELD POLYTRACK 1 August 2003 to 31 July 2005

Sire	W/R	%	Non-Handicap			Handicap			£1 Level Stake
			2yo	3yo	4yo+	2yo	3yo	4yo+	
Most Welcome	23-75	30.7	0-8	3-7	10-19	0-0	3-8	7-33	+129.10
Polar Falcon	19-142	13.4	2-13	1-14	1-29	1-6	7-27	7-53	+21.28
Efisio	18-121	14.9	2-11	2-13	2-21	0-1	3-12	9-63	+39.88
Grand Lodge	18-144	12.5	3-16	4-29	9-32	0-2	2-14	0-51	+10.40
Cadeaux Genereux	16-144	11.1	0-8	4-26	3-29	0-0	2-18	7-63	-32.74
Pursuit Of Love	16-146	11.0	2-6	3-28	3-40	1-2	2-16	5-54	-35.29
Mark Of Esteem	14-94	14.9	1-15	5-23	5-14	0-2	2-16	1-24	+1.68
First Trump	14-118	11.9	0-5	1-16	2-37	0-1	2-12	9-47	+25.50
Sri Pekan	14-125	11.2	1-7	1-22	3-32	0-0	1-10	8-54	-17.00
Indian Ridge	13-94	13.8	1-10	1-8	6-27	0-1	1-7	4-41	-14.25
Linamix	12-51	23.5	0-7	1-4	4-14	0-0	3-10	4-16	+6.45
Night Shift	12-156	7.7	1-14	2-19	2-48	1-5	1-27	5-43	-28.75
Piccolo	11-132	8.3	4-15	1-29	1-30	1-4	1-18	3-36	-57.75
Distant Relative	10-71	14.1	0-0	0-0	3-34	0-0	0-0	7-37	+51.00
Selkirk	10-75	13.3	2-6	1-22	1-16	0-1	4-9	2-21	+6.25
Spectrum	10-79	12.7	0-11	1-14	0-9	0-3	5-26	4-16	-22.67
Green Desert	10-87	11.5	1-9	2-12	1-20	0-1	0-8	6-37	+15.87
Magic Ring	10-97	10.3	0-3	0-10	6-39	0-1	1-10	3-34	+16.50
Mind Games	10-103	9.7	0-7	4-23	3-32	0-3	2-16	1-22	+11.88
Pivotal	10-104	9.6	0-12	2-15	6-23	1-2	0-12	1-40	-15.08
Tagula	10-106	9.4	0-13	1-17	3-21	0-0	2-25	4-30	-39.42
Barathea	10-120	8.3	0-4	5-20	3-51	0-0	0-19	2-26	-33.42
Rainbow Quest	9-39	23.1	0-3	1-7	1-8	0-0	1-1	6-20	+30.00
Royal Academy	9-49	18.4	0-0	2-7	2-11	0-0	0-1	5-30	+19.45
Desert Sun	9-51	17.6	1-7	5-25	0-0	2-4	1-7	0-8	+62.50
Soviet Star	9-70	12.9	3-18	2-11	1-11	0-2	3-18	0-10	-5.17
Marju	9-82	11.0	0-7	1-10	2-22	0-2	2-10	4-31	-16.75
Komaite	9-91	9.9	0-8	1-16	3-23	0-0	2-13	3-31	-27.75
Groom Dancer	9-96	9.4	2-18	4-21	1-18	1-5	0-11	1-23	-14.10
Vettori	9-104	8.7	3-19	0-19	2-12	1-6	0-22	3-26	-46.75

Sire	W/R	%	Non-Handicap			Handicap			£1 Level Stake
			2yo	3yo	4yo+	2yo	3yo	4yo+	
Danehill	9-106	8.5	1-7	1-14	3-25	0-0	0-14	4-46	-36.00
Mtoto	8-54	14.8	1-8	2-11	3-16	0-0	0-6	2-13	+12.25
Foxhound	8-65	12.3	4-12	1-20	2-9	0-2	1-17	0-5	+4.05
Atraf	8-81	9.9	1-9	4-31	1-7	0-3	1-19	1-12	-33.00
Royal Applause	8-108	7.4	3-16	1-28	0-17	0-2	1-17	3-28	-55.75
Compton Place	8-113	7.1	2-18	1-19	2-35	0-2	2-15	1-24	-70.50
Mujadil	8-86	9.3	0-12	3-15	1-15	0-3	1-16	3-25	+21.50
Bahamian Bounty	8-91	8.8	2-9	0-13	1-29	0-4	0-11	5-25	-21.25
King Of Kings	7-37	18.9	1-4	1-7	0-5	0-0	2-14	3-7	-1.12
Singspiel	7-44	15.9	3-9	2-9	1-9	0-1	0-5	1-11	+15.00
Lycius	7-49	14.3	0-0	1-3	5-14	0-0	0-3	1-29	-18.17
Desert Prince	7-52	13.5	2-15	3-10	1-9	0-0	0-8	1-10	-6.73
Muhtarram	7-53	13.2	0-2	1-10	4-13	0-1	0-4	2-23	-16.50
Elmaamul	7-62	11.3	0-0	1-4	3-24	0-0	0-5	3-29	-16.50
Desert Story	7-68	10.3	1-14	0-15	2-8	0-2	0-9	4-20	+12.45
Beveled	7-69	10.1	0-0	0-0	2-25	0-0	0-0	5-44	+25.00
Charnwood Forest	7-70	10.0	0-1	2-12	2-26	0-0	0-7	3-24	-31.27
Desert Style	7-88	8.0	1-13	2-31	0-9	0-0	3-19	1-16	-40.75
Fraam	7-107	6.5	2-13	0-27	3-24	1-3	1-16	0-24	-50.50

CHAPTER THREE

SOUTHWELL

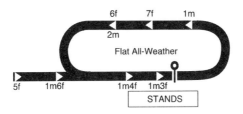

Address: Racecourse Office, Southwell Racecourse, Rolleston, Notts, NG25 0TS
Going & Doubtful weather: Racecourse Office: 01636 814481
Going: 01328 2388/0636

Location: Situated midway between the A1 and M1, Southwell Racecourse is easily accessible from most parts of the country.

How to get there: Road: Southwell Racecourse is situated 7 miles from Newark, with easy access from A1 and M1 via A46 and the A617.

Rail: Southwell Racecourse has an adjoining railway station at Rolleston. (Nottingham – Newark line).

Air: Helicopter landing and take-off facilities are available at Southwell. Please contact Mr David Williams on 07778 757680 for permission.

Clerk of the Course: Jon Pullin

Southwell will always hold a special place in my heart, as it was the first All-Weather track I ever visited in this country. The racecourse is set in quite an attractive part of the Nottinghamshire countryside and I always feel that when you are there during the winter, life slows down that little bit and everything is that much more relaxed.

The facilities at Southwell are excellent for what is perceived as a minor track, and put the facilities at some so-called Grade One tracks to shame. The main stand is modern and extremely comfortable, with excellent viewing of the track from each enclosure. There are a selection of bars and restaurants on each floor and there are also plenty of Tote windows available including in the Members' Lounge, which I strongly recommend. This area is large and comfortable and has excellent views of the track from the front, and of the paddock from the rear. Many people tend to base themselves here for the afternoon, but they don't miss out on much and it's an ideal situation to be in when the weather is bad. The chip shop beneath the smaller public stand serves food that any town's 'chippie' would be proud of, but if you are going to eat in there during the winter make sure you have a warm coat because the temperature inside is the same as it is outside!

Southwell Racecourse is pretty easy to get to, though the final couple of miles to reach the track itself can be a bit tricky if you don't know where you're going. I made a bit of a pig's ear of that first journey back in 1994, mainly due to my complete ignorance as to the geography of the area, and at one stage I was convinced I was going to end up in China.

The track is a left-handed oval of about ten furlongs and the surface is Fibresand. The All-Weather track lies outside the turf course with the run from the final bend to the winning post about three-and-a-half furlongs, which is by far the longest of the three sand tracks. As a result, Southwell tends to favour the more galloping types and with the surface being much the slowest of the three, the ability to see out the trip is very important. There is also a five-furlong straight track, which is currently unique in British All-Weather racing. Horses that have already proved they can show decent form at Southwell are worth watching out for when they return, especially as it's now the only Fibresand track in the country and the form shown here does not transfer too well to the Polytrack venues.

There are no particularly high-class races run at Southwell, though there are some valuable handicaps of which two currently take place at the New Year meeting. To be honest, the fare on offer at most Southwell meetings isn't going to set the pulse racing in terms of quality, and because the overall standard of the horses that run here remains modest, whilst the standard of animal racing on the Polytrack is ever upward, the gap between the quality of racing on the different surfaces tends to be widening. It would be unfair if Fibresand became the poor relation of the Polytrack and a few classier races at Southwell wouldn't come amiss. After all, you wouldn't downgrade a race on turf because it is being run on soft ground rather than fast. Of course with so many more moderate horses in training than good ones, there is never going to be a problem with field sizes at Southwell.

Apart from suiting galloping types, the ability to take a handy position is of paramount importance, especially in races up to a mile. It's generally not crucial to lead, though front-runners are favoured over some trips (more of that later), but it's very difficult to come from too far back over any distance, certainly not in the same way as you can at Lingfield. However, the most notable aspect of Southwell is a massive track bias, which makes it almost imperative to race down the middle of the track in the home straight. This bias has been around for quite some time now and I will assume that it remains until there is clear evidence that it has disappeared. Most of the jockeys seem to be aware of it, so much so that when the runners turn for home in races over six furlongs or more, they all move in a cluster to the middle of the track for the final dash for home.

When I say most jockeys seem aware of the bias, you will still see one or two try and make their efforts close to either the inside or outside rail. To be fair, they may have little choice if the centre of the track has become congested by other horses, or if their mounts are starting to hang. Evidence suggests that if you are going to switch wide for your effort, it's better to come stands' side than go far side, as the ground close to the inside rail seems to be much deeper and slower than elsewhere and has been for a number of years. Basically, if you notice that a horse hasn't been beaten that far despite having raced close to the inside rail all the way up the home straight, then stick him straight in your notebook!

The following pages show the statistics for Southwell. Firstly jockeys, trainers and favourites, followed by draw and front-runners.

JOCKEYS (1 January 2002 to 31 May 2005)			
	Total W-R	Per Cent	£1 Level Stake
A Culhane	46-418	11.0	−64.68
Dean McKeown	36-312	12.0	+2.05
J Quinn	34-378	9.0	−138.91
L Fletcher	34-367	9.0	−91.67
I Mongan	33-276	12.0	−85.84
R Winston	31-227	14.0	+18.77
B Reilly	30-154	19.0	+91.75
C Catlin	30-313	10.0	+19.61
Darren Williams	29-283	10.0	−68.84
D Mernagh	26-144	18.0	+63.05
P Makin	25-238	11.0	−40.84
Lisa Jones	24-197	12.0	+7.20
J Fanning	23-239	10.0	−49.84
M Fenton	22-196	11.0	−66.74
F Norton	21-227	9.0	−39.63
F Lynch	21-166	13.0	+9.63
P Hanagan	21-219	10.0	−74.92
G Gibbons	18-202	9.0	−119.72
J Bramhill	17-268	6.0	−0.04
S W Kelly	17-175	10.0	−70.96
S Whitworth	15-173	9.0	−53.47
J-P Guillambert	15-93	16.0	+11.62
S Sanders	14-71	20.0	−25.57
Martin Dwyer	14-75	19.0	−14.40
D Fox	14-120	12.0	−5.67
S Drowne	13-89	15.0	+9.46
L Enstone	13-167	8.0	−93.62
D Holland	12-82	15.0	−25.63
G Duffield	12-132	9.0	−63.88
K Dalgleish	12-159	8.0	−72.19
A Nicholls	11-180	6.0	−54.00
Dale Gibson	10-231	4.0	−154.67
J Mackay	10-118	8.0	−58.70
T P Queally	10-98	10.0	−18.78
J F McDonald	10-99	10.0	−22.38
M Tebbutt	9-97	9.0	−37.63
Kim Tinkler	9-148	6.0	−84.17
J Edmunds	9-139	6.0	−30.00
G Faulkner	9-58	16.0	−13.88
D Sweeney	9-119	8.0	−6.77
P J Scallan	9-59	15.0	+11.43
F P Ferris	9-111	8.0	−31.44
P Mulrennan	9-73	12.0	−25.20
D Tudhope	9-84	11.0	−6.50
R Fitzpatrick	8-171	5.0	−90.00
Dane O'Neill	8-101	8.0	−45.00
D Nolan	8-136	6.0	−95.50
Joanna Badger	8-164	5.0	−40.00
T Eaves	8-146	5.0	−50.50
C Haddon	8-81	10.0	−36.43

TRAINERS

	Total W-R	2yo Stks	3yo Stks	Other Stks	2yo H'caps	3yo H'caps	Other H'caps	App'ce	A'teurs	Per cent	£1 Level stake
T D Barron	75-345	9-23	7-22	25-121	0-6	8-26	22-124	4-18	0-5	21.7	+103.15
P A Blockley	42-243	3-19	4-24	21-91	3-7	2-14	5-73	1-7	3-8	17.3	+23.89
K A Ryan	40-251	6-34	3-25	10-67	2-5	0-17	18-88	1-8	0-7	15.9	+56.61
K R Burke	33-234	6-23	1-16	14-105	2-8	3-23	3-43	2-9	2-7	14.1	-32.43
P C Haslam	32-204	4-37	3-26	9-34	2-17	9-35	0-27	2-14	3-14	15.7	-37.77
B Smart	30-217	1-12	4-13	9-59	2-6	1-27	10-86	2-11	1-3	13.8	+61.53
Mrs N Macauley	25-377	1-10	0-19	11-135	0-3	1-10	9-159	1-21	2-20	6.6	-162.12
S R Bowring	24-312	2-10	0-21	11-134	2-4	1-15	6-98	2-20	0-10	7.7	-44.97
D Shaw	24-358	2-23	2-15	9-135	1-8	6-37	4-124	0-8	0-8	6.7	-194.81
N P Littmoden	20-130	3-9	5-19	5-37	0-6	3-16	4-31	0-6	0-6	15.4	+65.26
M J Polglase	20-335	3-26	1-14	6-126	0-9	2-28	7-118	1-12	0-2	6.0	-128.84
J Balding	18-227	0-5	0-7	11-113	0-2	1-6	6-89	0-3	0-2	7.9	-23.25
H Morrison	18-67	2-6	1-6	5-17	0-0	0-2	8-33	1-2	1-1	26.9	+16.69
Sir Mark Prescott	17-74	3-17	1-6	2-16	0-2	2-9	9-23	0-1	0-0	23.0	-24.57
D W Chapman	17-316	0-6	0-6	14-158	0-4	0-13	2-113	0-10	1-6	5.4	-169.42
R Hollinshead	17-241	2-12	1-17	7-96	0-6	1-15	5-80	0-13	1-2	7.1	-102.42
J A Osborne	15-96	2-25	3-11	5-27	1-9	1-6	2-17	1-1	0-0	15.6	-26.66
Mrs C A Dunnett	15-84	0-6	0-4	5-23	0-1	1-7	9-43	0-0	0-0	17.9	+46.00
R A Fahey	14-91	1-5	0-3	5-32	0-1	0-4	8-41	0-5	0-0	15.4	+10.75
B Ellison	13-77	1-1	0-2	1-19	0-0	1-1	6-43	0-1	4-10	16.9	+46.50
D Carroll	12-91	1-11	0-1	6-43	0-0	0-4	3-24	1-7	1-1	13.2	+16.00
W J Haggas	12-40	2-12	2-4	4-10	0-1	3-4	1-8	0-1	0-0	30.0	+29.14
R M H Cowell	12-113	1-20	1-7	5-34	0-0	0-10	5-39	0-3	0-0	10.6	+60.90
P Howling	11-127	0-5	0-4	6-61	0-1	0-2	5-49	0-4	0-1	8.7	-73.00
M C Chapman	11-270	0-11	2-15	4-117	1-5	1-20	3-78	0-16	0-8	4.1	-165.00
E J Alston	11-62	0-2	0-1	1-10	0-1	2-4	8-42	0-1	0-1	17.7	+0.42
P W Hiatt	11-110	0-2	1-4	3-39	0-0	1-2	3-45	3-13	0-5	10.0	+16.38
A Berry	11-249	4-43	3-29	1-97	1-6	0-16	2-47	0-7	0-4	4.4	-164.88
W J Musson	10-64	0-2	0-1	4-14	0-0	1-4	5-33	0-9	0-1	15.6	-6.53
B J Meehan	10-65	3-22	2-12	0-8	0-4	2-8	3-10	0-0	0-1	15.4	-22.61
S C Williams	10-48	0-2	1-4	4-18	0-1	1-8	3-12	0-0	1-3	20.8	+18.42

FAVOURITES			
	W-R	Per cent	£1 Level stake
2yo Stks	40-109	36.7	−1.56
3yo Stks	39-88	44.3	+11.45
3yo+ Stks	165-536	30.8	−29.00
Totals	244-733	33.3	−19.11
2yo H'caps	11-24	45.8	+16.09
3yo H'caps	24-101	23.8	−24.85
3yo+ H'caps	127-514	24.7	−60.66
Totals	162-639	25.4	−69.42
App'ce	18-56	32.1	−0.41
Amateurs	12-38	31.6	+2.97
Totals	30-94	31.9	+2.56
All Favs	436-1466	29.7	−85.97

I have to admit that the draw stats for five furlongs did cause me a bit of a headache. I noticed a couple of years ago that those horses starting from the lowest stalls over the straight five were doing rather well, which is borne out by the statistics shown, but then for a short period they didn't do so well, usually when they were carrying my money! I couldn't understand it, because otherwise the track seemed to be riding the same way as normal. I had a good think about it and now I'm pretty sure I have solved the mystery.

The answer is that, unlike with just about every other start on Britain's All-Weather tracks, on Southwell's five furlong course stall one, for instance, is not always in the same place, whereas over six furlongs stall one is always closest to the inside rail. What I mean is, in a seven-strong field over five furlongs, stall seven would be tight against the stands' rail, whilst in a 14-runner field stall seven would be aiming right down the centre of the track. Horses starting from that stall would be taking significantly different routes in each race, even though both will have started from stall seven.

In his book *Betting For A Living* (Aesculus Press, 1992) Nick Mordin advocates turning the stall numbers on their head in order to assess the statistics for when the stalls are placed next to a right-hand rail. If you do that for Southwell's straight five furlongs, you get the statistics on page 45.

SOUTHWELL DRAW AND FRONT-RUNNER STATISTICS
1 August 2003 to 31 July 2005

5 furlongs

Draw Pos	Winners	%
Low	34	33
Middle	37	36
High	32	31

Draw No	Runners	Winners	%
1	99	16	16
2	97	11	11
3	100	7	7
4	98	6	6
5	98	7	7
6	98	11	11
7	96	12	13
8	91	4	4
9	82	5	6
10	80	4	5
11	66	9	14
12	49	1	2
13	43	3	7
14	37	5	14
15	16	1	6
16	15	1	7

Front Runners Impact Value = 3.0
28 winners from 103 races (27%)

7 furlongs

Draw Pos	Winners	%
Low	27	20
Middle	65	47
High	45	33

Draw No	Runners	Winners	%
1	130	7	5
2	134	8	6
3	129	9	7
4	130	12	9
5	130	22	17
6	133	18	14
7	130	13	10
8	121	9	7
9	106	8	8
10	95	10	11
11	76	4	5
12	73	5	7
13	60	7	12
14	48	2	4
15	21	2	10
16	15	1	7

Front Runners Impact Value = 1.2
16 winners from 137 races (12%)

6 furlongs

Draw Pos	Winners	%
Low	47	29
Middle	58	36
High	56	35

Draw No	Runners	Winners	%
1	153	9	6
2	156	18	12
3	156	15	10
4	150	15	10
5	149	16	11
6	154	9	6
7	153	12	8
8	137	14	10
9	136	14	10
10	123	10	8
11	107	9	8
12	87	8	9
13	74	2	3
14	60	7	12
15	23	2	9
16	20	1	5

Front Runners Impact Value = 1.5
22 winners from 161 races (14%)

1 mile

Draw Pos	Winners	%
Low	45	24
Middle	71	38
High	73	39

Draw No	Runners	Winners	%
1	177	10	6
2	180	20	11
3	180	12	7
4	178	16	9
5	184	22	12
6	180	16	9
7	175	9	5
8	159	15	9
9	146	14	10
10	142	20	14
11	111	10	9
12	96	10	10
13	80	5	6
14	74	8	11
15	29	1	3

Front Runners Impact Value = 1.1
21 winners from 189 races (11%)

1 mile 3 furlongs

Draw Pos	Winners	%
Low	16	29
Middle	23	41
High	17	30

Draw No	Runners	Winners	%
1	51	9	18
2	52	3	6
3	52	5	10
4	54	11	20
5	51	2	4
6	54	6	11
7	50	4	8
8	47	6	13
9	40	5	13
10	32	0	0
11	23	2	9
12	20	1	5
13	15	2	13
14	15	0	0
15	5	0	0
16	4	0	0

Front Runners Impact Value = 1.9
11 winners from 56 races (20%)

1 mile 4 furlongs

Draw Pos	Winners	%
Low	21	26
Middle	28	34
High	33	40

Draw No	Runners	Winners	%
1	79	4	5
2	77	11	14
3	76	8	11
4	80	8	10
5	77	7	9
6	76	10	13
7	71	8	11
8	67	8	12
9	57	6	11
10	46	2	4
11	31	2	6
12	25	3	12
13	24	2	8
14	21	0	0
15	9	0	0
16	8	3	38

Front Runners Impact Value = 0.8
7 winners from 82 races (9%)

1 mile 6 furlongs

Draw Pos	Winners	%
Low	6	18
Middle	16	47
High	12	35

Draw No	Runners	Winners	%
1	33	1	3
2	32	3	9
3	32	4	13
4	32	7	22
5	29	2	7
6	29	2	7
7	30	1	3
8	24	6	25
9	22	2	9
10	20	4	20
11	17	1	6
12	12	1	8
13	9	0	0
14	5	0	0
15	3	0	0
16	2	0	0

Front Runners Impact Value = 0.3
1 winner from 34 races (3%)

2 miles

Draw Pos	Winners	%
Low	7	32
Middle	9	41
High	6	27

Draw No	Runners	Winners	%
1	21	2	10
2	22	2	9
3	21	4	19
4	20	1	5
5	21	1	5
6	20	3	15
7	18	4	22
8	21	2	10
9	17	2	12
10	12	0	0
11	6	1	17
12	5	0	0
13	4	0	0
14	3	0	0
15	2	0	0
16	2	0	0

Front Runners Impact Value = 0.0
0 winners from 22 races (0%)

INVERTED DRAW STATISTICS FOR 5 FURLONGS

Draw Pos	Winners	%
Stands Side	32	31
Middle	37	36
Far Side	34	33

Pos Away From Nearside Rail	Runners	Winners	%
1	100	11	11
2	97	5	5
3	96	9	9
4	99	14	14
5	95	8	8
6	96	10	10
7	94	11	12
8	92	6	7
9	84	7	8
10	72	9	13
11	61	6	10
12	47	2	4
13	38	2	5
14	30	2	7
15	16	1	6
16	9	0	0

This does make things a bit clearer. Notice how the number of runners drops away sharply once you reach nine positions or more away from the stands' rail. This means there are relatively few races run over this trip with eight runners or less. The inference is that horses starting from real stall one in fields of up to 11 runners (up to 11 positions away from the stands' rail) tend to do well, but in fields of 12 or more they are going to be racing closer to the dreaded far rail and that is definitely where I did my money.

In races on the round course, the closer to the first bend you are the more desirable it is to be drawn low. This is not because the inside rail is favoured, not a bit of it. It's because horses from these stalls often reach the first bend near the front, and then have the freedom to manoeuvre off the inside rail and occupy the faster strip down the middle of the track whilst racing up with the pace. Over trips with a longer run to the first bend, there is more time for those drawn wide to be in a handier position when the first bend is reached and the statistics therefore become more random. Despite that, notice how bad the record is of the very highest and lowest stalls over trips from six furlongs to a mile.

As far as front-runners are concerned, the IV for the straight five furlongs is the largest for any distance at the three All-Weather tracks and

I believe it's safe to say that horses that like to come from off the pace might as well stay at home. In fact the IV is so favourable to front-runners, that if after analysing the running styles of all horses in any given race you have identified one that is likely to gain an uncontested lead, that horse is worthy of support in its own right.

The bias falls away as race distance increases, except for increasing again slightly for races over one mile three furlongs, largely due I'm sure to the proximity of the start to the first bend.

Even though it's difficult to come from a long way back at Southwell, it's also extremely difficult to make all the running over the longer distances. Fibresand is a very testing surface and it requires a great deal of stamina to truly see out the extended trips under any circumstances, but trying to make all is an even tougher assignment and up until now it has proved beyond the capabilities of most.

Finally, on the next page is a list of the most successful sires on the Southwell Fibresand between August 2003 and July 2005.

SIRES WHOSE PROGENY HAVE WON MORE THAN FIVE RACES ON THE SOUTHWELL FIBRESAND 1 August 2003 to 31 July 2005

Sire	W/R	%	Non-Handicap			Handicap			£1 Level Stake
			2yo	3yo	4yo+	2yo	3yo	4yo+	
Night Shift	19-152	12.5	1-8	2-12	8-67	0-3	2-10	6-52	+2.08
Komaite	16-138	11.6	5-20	1-21	6-42	1-3	0-11	4-41	-6.55
Forzando	14-90	15.6	1-7	2-5	7-43	1-2	0-8	3-25	+20.42
Piccolo	14-101	13.9	0-2	1-7	6-30	0-1	4-18	3-43	+34.25
Wolfhound	13-99	13.1	1-4	2-16	8-42	0-1	1-9	1-27	-20.16
Distant View	12-70	17.1	0-2	1-5	3-14	0-0	0-2	8-47	+16.25
Orpen	10-61	16.4	1-10	3-18	0-9	1-6	5-16	0-2	-13.97
Efisio	10-79	12.7	0-6	3-7	0-21	0-1	0-8	7-36	-6.28
Magic Ring	10-87	11.5	0-2	0-6	3-34	0-0	0-5	7-40	+18.46
Mujadil	10-89	11.2	0-4	2-4	3-29	0-5	1-12	4-35	+37.50
Pivotal	9-56	16.1	0-1	1-3	3-21	0-2	0-2	5-27	-19.50
Mark Of Esteem	9-60	15.0	1-9	1-7	2-13	0-3	2-8	3-20	+4.40
Royal Applause	9-72	12.5	0-5	2-17	1-24	2-2	2-9	2-15	+0.73
Selkirk	8-56	14.3	0-1	1-3	4-29	0-1	2-7	1-15	-22.84
Bishop Of Cashel	8-62	12.9	0-5	0-4	3-10	0-0	0-6	5-37	-14.50
Bahhare	7-26	26.9	0-1	3-5	0-7	0-0	1-7	3-6	+22.93
Marju	7-27	25.9	1-1	1-2	3-7	0-0	1-6	1-11	+24.58
Fasliyev	7-29	24.1	0-5	2-7	2-4	1-4	2-5	0-4	+2.00
Desert Sun	7-34	20.6	2-12	2-6	2-3	0-3	1-8	0-2	+5.13
Polar Prince	7-38	18.4	1-2	1-7	3-11	0-3	1-5	1-10	+12.50
Up And At 'Em	7-38	18.4	0-1	3-8	1-13	0-1	0-1	3-14	-6.27
Grand Lodge	7-43	16.3	0-2	1-5	3-19	0-0	1-10	2-7	-8.47
Petong	7-53	13.2	0-6	0-3	3-24	0-0	0-1	4-19	-3.00
Paris House	7-55	12.7	2-16	0-12	1-11	1-1	0-6	3-9	-11.50
Charnwood Forest	7-65	10.8	1-1	2-12	1-17	0-2	0-11	3-22	-9.92
Victory Note	7-68	10.3	0-2	2-9	1-27	0-3	1-15	3-12	-4.25
Cadeaux Genereux	7-78	9.0	0-2	0-4	6-33	0-0	0-4	1-35	-40.27
Starborough	6-17	35.3	1-1	0-0	1-1	0-0	0-5	4-10	+22.25
Sure Blade	6-22	27.3	0-2	0-0	2-5	1-2	0-1	3-12	+14.71

Sire	W/R	%	Non-Handicap				Handicap			£1 Level Stake
			2yo	3yo	4yo+	2yo	3yo	4yo+		
Most Welcome	6-38	15.8	0-3	0-4	5-13	0-1	0-0	1-17	-13.27
Priolo	6-43	14.0	0-1	0-1	5-26	0-0	0-0	1-15	-27.05
Wizard King	6-61	9.8	1-8	3-19	2-18	0-1	0-6	0-9	-9.00
Emperor Jones	6-73	8.2	0-3	0-0	5-35	0-0	0-5	1-30	-32.25
First Trump	6-74	8.1	0-11	0-6	2-30	0-0	0-6	4-21	-28.80
Sri Pekan	6-78	7.7	1-7	1-16	2-25	0-0	1-7	1-23	-40.75
Mind Games	6-94	6.4	1-17	2-19	2-29	1-4	0-14	0-11	-29.50

CHAPTER FOUR

WOLVERHAMPTON

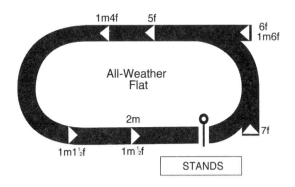

Address: Wolverhampton Racecourse, Gorsebrook Road, Wolverhampton, WV6 0PE
Going & Doubtful weather: Office: 01902 390020

Location: Located less than 2 miles from the centre of Wolverhampton, the Racecourse has excellent access to the M6 and M54.

How to get there: Road: Located off the A449 dual carriageway. Follow signs to Dunstall Park

Rail: Trains from London Euston to Wolverhampton Station, which is just 2 miles from the Racecourse.

Air: Flights to Birmingham International Airport which is situated approximately 25 miles from Wolverhampton.

Clerk of the Course: Fergus Cameron

There is nothing quite like a Saturday night at Wolverhampton, and a few years ago I could never imagine myself saying that. I fell in love with the racecourse the first time I went there and that love affair has lasted ever since. The facilities are absolutely superb for what is still regarded as a minor track, with a huge modern grandstand containing bars, restaurants and everything you could possibly need for a comfortable and enjoyable day or night at the races. I would still single out the Zongalero

Restaurant on the top floor of the grandstand as an experience to be sampled, if only because it's the only restaurant I regularly frequent, but there are others which I am sure are just as excellent.

With more and more tracks installing similar panoramic restaurants, a larger number of people will now be familiar with the concept of enjoying the racing spectacle whilst consuming a three- or four-course meal, but a Saturday evening meeting in the Zongalero remains a true pleasure and will continue to appeal to those who don't necessarily have a great interest in racing, but want to be entertained and have a bit of fun. Witnessing a floodlit meeting is quite an experience if you have never tried it before, as the track takes on the look of a theatre stage on which the stars are the horses. Of course it always helps if your selection wins!

For a very reasonable price, you get entrance to the course, a decent three-course meal and your own table for the evening with its own television, plus a wonderful view of the track. My first experience of the Zongalero Restaurant reminded me of the facilities I came across whilst in America, where the well-being and comfort of the racegoer is paramount. Wolverhampton should be applauded for that.

At the moment the track is in a unique position of being able to stage floodlit racing, which means that the legendary Saturday evening meetings outside the core evening racing schedule continue to flourish, but the floodlit monopoly will end when Kempton and Great Leighs open up for business next year. Hopefully these three tracks will stage fixtures that will complement each other rather than compete with one another, which can be to no-one's benefit.

As I have said, the Saturday evening fixtures at Dunstall Park are hugely popular, proving that if you put on decent entertainment, people will turn up. On the other hand, the course is rather a lonely place on a midweek afternoon in the depths of winter, but I like the place so much it doesn't bother me. I just have more room in which to roam.

Thanks to the motorway system, Wolverhampton is pretty easy to get to, though the roads in the immediate vicinity of the track can be extremely congested during the afternoon rush hour, as can the M6 near Birmingham. If you don't fancy getting caught up in all of that, or don't fancy a long drive home after the last race at an evening meeting, there is always the Garden Court Hotel which is attached to the back of the grandstand complex.

The track itself is nearly a mile in circumference, with a run-in from the final bend of just under two furlongs. Following one or two problems with the old Fibresand, the surface was replaced with Polytrack, which has been in operation since October 2004 and, as was the case with Lingfield, the new surface has been greeted with almost universal praise. The other similarity with Lingfield of course, is that punters have found themselves having to learn the idiosyncratic nature of what is basically a brand new track. The old Fibresand statistics had to be thrown out of the window, as it soon became pretty obvious that Wolverhampton had lost its label of possessing one of the most pronounced track biases in the country.

On the old Fibresand, if you raced next to the inside rail for any length of time, in 95% of races you would literally be sunk. The surface became very slow on the inside, especially on the bends where the camber caused the sand particles to roll down the hill and make the surface very deep. Now however, there is no problem with racing tight against the inside rail, not because the ground there is any faster than on the outside, but simply because it's the shortest way home.

It's now incredibly difficult to win if you go too wide on the bends (the polar opposite of the old Fibresand where you couldn't go wide enough!) and if you spot a horse that has managed to win or finish close up having gone more than six horse-widths wide on the home bend, they should be noted.

In many cases it has proved to be a major advantage to stick as close as possible to the inside rail for as long as possible, providing of course you can get a clear run, and already one or two jockeys have sussed out the best way to ride this track and have used that knowledge to their advantage (more of that in Chapter Eight).

One thing hasn't changed though. In the old days, form shown at Wolverhampton was no guarantee that a horse would show the same level of form at Southwell, simply because both surfaces were Fibresand. The same is now true with Wolverhampton and Lingfield, even though both are Polytrack. The conformations of these two tracks are totally different, but even more relevant is that a study of race times has shown the Polytrack surface at Wolverhampton to be slower than at Lingfield. In fact Wolverhampton fits in almost exactly between Lingfield and Southwell in terms of average times, which is an important factor to take into consideration when assessing the chances of a horse running here after performing at another sand venue.

Wolverhampton used to stage a Listed contest during December, the Wulfrun Stakes, which was the first race of its class to be run on sand in this country. It only lasted four years and was won by Prince Of Andros in 1995 and 1996, Farmost (beating Running Stag) in 1997 and by Refuse To Lose in 1998. Unfortunately, the loss of revenue caused by the reduction in Saturday evening meetings at the end of the 90s caused the race's demise, and Wolverhampton also ceased to hold the valuable Weatherbys Dash, a race run in August and restricted to two-year-olds bought at the Dunstall Park Breeze-Up Sales earlier in the year.

There are still some decent prizes up for grabs though, of which the biggest is the £50,000 Lincoln Trial held in the middle of March. In its early years the contest proved a decent pointer to the Lincoln itself with Kuala Lipis (fourth in 1997) and John Ferneley (third in 2000) both going on to win the big Doncaster handicap, whilst the 1999 winner Captain Scott went on to chase home Right Wing at Town Moor.

In 2001, because it was shown that so many horses wanted to run in the Lincoln Trial, certainly more than the safety limit of 13 would allow, Wolverhampton staged a sort of Lincoln Trial consolation race for those horses who just missed out on the main event. The race was won by Nimello, who then went on to win the Lincoln itself exactly two weeks later.

The Wolverhampton Polytrack may still be in its infancy, but already there are signs that the bigger trainers are running some of their better younger horses on the surface, rather like happened at Lingfield, and that can only be good for the future quality of the racing at Dunstall Park.

The following pages show the relevant statistics for the Wolverhampton Polytrack, covering jockeys, trainers and favourites, followed by the draw and front-runners.

JOCKEYS (2 October 2004 to 31 May2005)

Total	Per W-R	£1 Level Cent	Stake
N Callan	30-207	14.0	−12.30
E Ahern	29-143	20.0	−12.17
C Catlin	25-174	14.0	**+67.33**
A Culhane	21-195	11.0	−29.50
R Winston	20-153	13.0	−28.45
S W Kelly	17-208	8.0	**+21.95**
P Hanagan	17-176	10.0	−43.00
J Quinn	16-164	10.0	−45.92
G Baker	14-98	14.0	**+27.75**
T Eaves	11-88	13.0	**+35.50**
P P Mathers	11-119	9.0	**+1.50**
J-P Guillambert	11-82	13.0	−24.80
K Fallon	10-41	24.0	**+1.12**
F Norton	10-117	9.0	−36.50
D Sweeney	10-111	9.0	**+14.75**
S Drowne	9-124	7.0	−75.52
C Haddon	9-52	17.0	**+35.00**
J Fortune	8-53	15.0	−4.84
Dane O'Neill	8-85	9.0	−13.75
J F Egan	7-84	8.0	−28.13
M Fenton	7-73	10.0	−1.75
O Urbina	7-45	16.0	**+20.50**
I Mongan	7-80	9.0	−36.17
B Reilly	7-72	10.0	−17.42
D Fox	7-30	23.0	**+25.00**
P Makin	7-116	6.0	−60.63
D Tudhope	7-40	18.0	**+17.50**
A Kirby	7-56	13.0	−20.52
J Fanning	6-103	6.0	−51.00
Martin Dwyer	6-56	11.0	−35.33
T P Queally	6-122	5.0	−63.50
R Kingscote	6-36	17.0	**+37.50**
S Whitworth	5-88	6.0	−16.00
L Dettori	5-18	28.0	+7.75
S Sanders	5-41	12.0	-2.50
F Lynch	5-30	17.0	-7.50
N Chalmers	5-67	7.0	-13.80
Lisa Jones	5-66	8.0	+25.00
A Quinn	5-49	10.0	-24.79
Dean McKeown	4-76	5.0	-50.09
Darren Williams	4-90	4.0	-52.25
R Thomas	4-36	11.0	-4.50
G Gibbons	4-33	12.0	+15.41
D Allan	4-61	7.0	-43.75
L P Keniry	4-58	7.0	+13.00
J F McDonald	4-63	6.0	-40.27
N Mackay	4-48	8.0	-30.82
R Kennemore	4-12	33.0	+27.00
Dale Gibson	3-39	8.0	-13.00
T Quinn	3-49	6.0	-36.25
A Daly	3-72	4.0	-54.50

TRAINERS

	Total W-R	2yo Stks	3yo Stks	Other Stks	2yo H'caps	3yo H'caps	Other H'caps	App'ce	A'teurs	Per cent	£1 Level stake
W M Brisbourne	24-197	0-4	0-1	13-82	0-0	0-1	9-91	1-14	1-4	12.2	-22.88
A W Carroll	22-139	0-2	3-12	7-54	0-1	0-1	9-53	1-8	2-8	15.8	+75.00
P A Blockley	12-128	1-14	1-17	7-42	1-6	0-4	1-34	1-3	0-8	9.4	-51.51
Miss G Kelleway	10-89	0-1	0-8	8-47	0-0	1-2	1-23	0-4	0-4	11.2	-22.42
R A Fahey	10-80	0-5	1-8	2-24	1-2	1-5	4-32	0-1	1-3	12.5	-27.38
M R Channon	9-45	1-10	1-6	4-12	0-5	0-4	3-8	0-0	0-0	20.0	+20.50
D R Loder	9-35	2-7	3-15	2-5	0-0	0-6	2-2	0-0	0-0	25.7	+3.50
N P Littmoden	9-63	2-9	1-4	3-22	0-0	0-3	1-18	1-2	1-5	14.3	-21.38
J A Osborne	9-60	5-17	1-12	2-7	0-8	0-3	0-12	0-0	1-1	15.0	-7.75
R Hollinshead	8-91	0-3	0-7	4-42	0-2	0-1	4-29	0-5	0-2	8.8	-27.50
K A Ryan	8-72	0-4	0-10	2-16	0-6	0-4	5-31	0-0	1-1	11.1	-36.37
Stef Liddiard	8-89	0-2	0-1	4-36	0-1	0-2	4-47	0-0	0-0	9.0	-29.38
S R Bowring	7-48	0-2	0-2	0-10	0-0	0-1	5-28	2-3	0-2	14.6	+12.50
I Semple	7-61	0-0	0-3	2-16	0-0	0-3	5-37	0-1	0-1	11.5	-11.50
P Howling	6-77	1-3	0-3	3-38	0-0	1-2	1-31	0-0	0-0	7.8	-24.00
J M Bradley	6-82	0-1	1-8	0-33	0-3	1-2	2-26	1-8	1-1	7.3	-5.50
Mrs N Macauley	6-55	0-2	0-6	2-27	0-0	0-1	4-15	0-2	0-2	10.9	-2.50
P D Evans	6-116	0-13	1-9	3-53	0-3	0-5	1-23	1-1	0-9	5.2	-77.50
C A Dwyer	6-67	0-6	1-12	5-30	0-2	0-3	0-12	0-1	0-1	9.0	-26.75
E A L Dunlop	6-19	3-7	0-1	0-3	1-1	1-4	1-3	0-0	0-0	31.6	+6.75
J Noseda	6-15	0-0	3-6	1-5	1-1	1-2	0-1	0-0	0-0	40.0	+9.09
G A Butler	6-36	3-8	0-5	1-9	0-2	0-3	2-9	0-0	0-0	16.7	-2.87
S Kirk	6-51	2-10	1-1	0-9	1-7	0-2	2-22	0-0	0-0	11.8	+1.63
W R Swinburn	6-24	0-1	0-1	1-8	0-0	0-0	5-14	0-0	0-0	25.0	+7.33
B W Hills	5-22	1-1	1-3	2-4	0-0	0-3	1-11	0-0	0-0	22.7	-4.25
K R Burke	5-50	1-5	0-6	2-19	0-5	0-1	2-9	0-1	0-4	10.0	-25.25
Mrs L Stubbs	5-30	2-3	0-1	1-13	0-0	0-2	1-7	1-4	0-0	16.7	-8.25
C R Egerton	5-17	0-0	1-1	2-3	0-1	0-1	2-11	0-0	0-0	29.4	+7.00
J G Given	5-44	1-11	1-5	0-8	1-1	1-3	1-16	0-0	0-0	11.4	+10.50
R P Elliott	5-54	0-13	1-6	2-16	1-4	0-2	0-11	1-2	0-0	9.3	+9.75
A Bailey	4-47	0-5	1-8	1-14	0-3	1-3	0-8	0-3	1-3	8.5	+7.00

FAVOURITES

	W-R	Per cent	£1 Level stake
2yo Stks	25-65	38.5	+8.36
3yo Stks	16-56	28.6	−6.52
3yo+ Stks	61-230	26.5	−18.24
Totals	102-351	29.1	−16.40
2yo H'caps	4-21	19.0	−7.50
3yo H'caps	10-29	34.5	+9.13
3yo+ H'caps	48-224	21.4	−36.90
Totals	62-274	22.6	−35.27
App'ce	2-22	9.1	−17.38
Amateurs	3-19	15.8	−7.62
Totals	5-41	12.2	−25.00
All Favs	169-666	25.4	−76.67

WOLVERHAMPTON DRAW AND FRONT-RUNNER STATISTICS
2 October 2004 to 31 July 2005

5 furlongs 20 yards

Draw Pos	Winners	%
Low	31	48
Middle	17	26
High	17	26

Draw No	Runners	Winners	%
1	64	10	16
2	63	12	19
3	64	5	8
4	60	6	10
5	65	8	12
6	60	4	7
7	62	2	3
8	61	1	2
9	60	5	8
10	60	5	8
11	56	2	4
12	51	1	2
13	40	4	10

Front Runners Impact Value = 2.7
18 winners from 65 races (28%)

5 furlongs 216 yards

Draw Pos	Winners	%
Low	48	44
Middle	34	31
High	26	24

Draw No	Runners	Winners	%
1	106	20	19
2	105	6	6
3	104	12	12
4	103	15	15
5	103	11	11
6	100	9	9
7	104	3	3
8	99	7	7
9	99	7	7
10	93	4	4
11	85	6	7
12	83	6	7
13	77	2	3

Front Runners Impact Value = 1.9
25 winners from 108 races (23%)

7 furlongs 32 yards

Draw Pos	Winners	%
Low	55	44
Middle	43	34
High	28	22

Draw No	Runners	Winners	%
1	119	15	13
2	123	13	11
3	121	19	16
4	114	13	11
5	121	8	7
6	122	8	7
7	120	10	8
8	117	15	13
9	114	5	4
10	111	5	5
11	107	8	7
12	96	7	7

Front Runners Impact Value = 1.3
18 winners from 126 races (14%)

1 mile 1f 103yds

Draw Pos	Winners	%
Low	30	33
Middle	31	34
High	29	32

Draw No	Runners	Winners	%
1	86	10	12
2	86	9	10
3	86	7	8
4	87	5	6
5	85	7	8
6	84	6	7
7	87	10	11
8	88	9	10
9	84	5	6
10	82	6	7
11	78	6	8
12	65	5	8
13	59	5	8

Front Runners Impact Value = 1.0
9 winners from 90 races (10%)

1 mile 141 yards

Draw Pos	Winners	%
Low	49	36
Middle	46	34
High	40	30

Draw No	Runners	Winners	%
1	130	8	6
2	130	22	17
3	134	9	7
4	130	13	10
5	132	11	8
6	126	6	5
7	129	10	8
8	123	13	11
9	128	12	9
10	120	5	4
11	113	2	2
12	103	14	14
13	96	10	10

Front Runners Impact Value = 0.9
13 winners from 135 races (10%)

1 mile 4f 50 yds

Draw Pos	Winners	%
Low	31	42
Middle	17	23
High	25	34

Draw No	Runners	Winners	%
1	71	11	15
2	69	6	9
3	72	9	13
4	68	9	13
5	68	4	6
6	70	4	6
7	72	5	7
8	65	7	11
9	66	5	8
10	59	6	10
11	53	4	8
12	49	3	6

Front Runners Impact Value = 1.9
14 winners from 73 races (19%)

1 mile 5f 194yds

Draw Pos	Winners	%
Low	4	18
Middle	12	55
High	6	27

Draw No	Runners	Winners	%
1	18	1	6
2	21	0	0
3	22	1	5
4	20	3	15
5	21	3	14
6	21	5	24
7	21	3	14
8	20	1	5
9	19	1	5
10	20	2	10
11	20	0	0
12	19	0	0
13	19	2	11

Front Runners Impact Value = 0.9
2 winners from 22 races (9%)

2 miles 119 yards

Draw Pos	Winners	%
Low	8	50
Middle	6	38
High	2	13

Draw No	Runners	Winners	%
1	16	2	13
2	16	6	38
3	14	0	0
4	15	0	0
5	15	2	13
6	16	2	13
7	14	1	7
8	13	1	8
9	15	0	0
10	14	0	0
11	14	1	7
12	11	0	0
13	9	1	11

Front Runners Impact Value = 0.0
0 winners from 16 races (0%)

As was the case when Lingfield replaced its surface with Polytrack, the draw statistics for Wolverhampton have been completely transformed and any preconceived ideas about where you want to be drawn based on the old Fibresand can be forgotten.

The advantage held by the lower draws between five to seven furlongs is striking, especially when you look at the percentage of winners to runners from each stall, and also illustrates how much of an advantage it now is to race close to the inside rail, especially rounding the home bend where the ground lost by racing too wide can be an insurmountable handicap.

The stats for eight and nine furlongs are fairly random and suggest you can win from just about anywhere, but over 12 furlongs the bias towards those drawn low returns to some degree. This, I believe, is more to do with the proximity of the start to the first bend, but unlike over the extended one mile where the start is also close to the first bend, there isn't a mad early dash from those drawn on the outside to take a handy position. Instead they are happy to tuck in behind the lower-drawn horses, rather than use up vital energy too early.

There haven't been enough races run over the very longest trips yet to come to any firm conclusions, despite the rather curious strike-rate of horses drawn in stall two over the extended two miles!

When it comes to front-runners, the stats rather back up the view of the naked eye that it is a big advantage to race up with the pace over sprint trips and that, combined with a low draw, is an extremely potent combination. An example of just how valuable this information proved to be on a personal level appears in Chapter Six.

The effectiveness of front-runners gradually subsides as distances lengthen, as it does at all three tracks, before disappearing altogether. Except that is, for the same glitch over 12 furlongs that was evident with the draw statistics. If you think about it, if a horse can get out quickly from a low draw in front without being hassled over this trip, and then race close to the inside rail around three long sweeping bends, he is going to save an awful lot of ground on a course where there is no track bias. His rivals will therefore have to come wide in order to overhaul him.

To end with, on the following page is a list of the top sires on the Wolverhampton Polytrack between October 2004 and July 2005.

SIRES WHOSE PROGENY HAVE WON MORE THAN FOUR RACES ON THE WOLVERHAMPTON POLYTRACK 2 October 2004 to 31 July 2005

Sire	W/R	%	Non-Handicap			Handicap			£1 Level Stake
			2yo	3yo	4yo+	2yo	3yo	4yo+	
Spectrum	12-76	15.8	4-18	1-19	1-16	0-2	2-10	4-11	−13.25
Danehill	9-59	15.3	0-3	2-5	3-16	0-0	1-3	3-32	+4.25
Grand Lodge	9-70	12.9	2-6	1-12	4-21	0-1	1-13	1-17	−13.37
Fasliyev	8-43	18.6	1-5	4-18	1-6	1-2	1-6	0-6	+12.75
Tagula	8-49	16.3	2-11	1-5	0-5	0-4	2-6	3-18	+4.00
Bahamian Bounty	8-53	15.1	0-6	2-8	0-12	1-4	0-5	5-18	+15.87
Mujadil	8-83	9.6	0-3	0-7	0-11	0-3	2-17	6-42	0.00
Josr Algarhoud	7-42	16.7	1-12	4-16	0-0	0-7	2-7	0-0	+27.25
Robellino	7-52	13.5	0-6	0-9	3-16	0-2	0-2	4-17	+17.75
Vettori	7-53	13.2	1-4	2-12	0-12	0-1	0-11	4-13	+24.00
Marju	7-54	13.0	0-7	2-3	1-13	0-4	1-6	3-21	+37.00
Barathea	7-56	12.5	2-4	0-7	2-18	0-0	0-5	3-22	+7.00
Green Desert	7-57	12.3	0-1	0-4	4-16	0-0	0-3	3-23	+1.00
Efisio	7-57	12.3	0-6	3-8	0-16	0-1	2-8	2-17	−8.00
Piccolo	7-95	7.4	2-6	0-15	1-21	0-3	0-8	4-42	−25.13
Second Empire	6-28	21.4	0-3	2-9	2-3	0-0	1-5	1-8	+28.06
Selkirk	6-35	17.1	0-1	1-3	3-19	0-0	0-1	2-11	+12.50
Bahhare	6-39	15.4	0-3	1-2	2-13	0-0	1-4	2-17	+3.25
Machiavellian	6-54	11.1	0-1	0-6	2-12	0-0	0-2	4-33	−7.00
Forzando	6-59	10.2	2-12	0-7	2-25	0-2	0-1	2-12	−10.34
Inchinor	6-73	8.2	1-8	0-11	4-23	0-3	0-6	1-22	−37.63
Komaite	6-81	7.4	0-4	2-14	1-15	0-4	1-13	2-31	−39.25
Lear Fan	5-14	35.7	0-1	2-3	1-3	0-0	1-1	1-6	+1.63
Key Of Luck	5-24	20.8	0-3	1-5	2-6	0-0	1-7	1-3	+30.07
Indian Rocket	5-26	19.2	0-1	1-5	3-10	0-1	0-2	1-7	+14.00
Perugino	5-32	15.6	0-1	1-6	2-11	1-1	0-0	1-13	+54.88
Polar Prince	5-35	14.3	0-0	0-4	3-9	0-2	0-1	2-19	−9.50
Ashkalani	5-37	13.5	0-0	1-5	0-9	0-0	0-4	4-19	+27.00
Desert Sun	5-41	12.2	1-5	3-13	1-2	0-2	0-12	0-7	−16.25

Sire	W/R	%	Non-Handicap			Handicap			£1 Level Stake
			2yo	3yo	4yo+	2yo	3yo	4yo+	
Groom Dancer	5-43	11.6	1-13	0-10	1-3	0-0	0-8	3-9	**+3.50**
Woodborough	5-43	11.6	1-6	0-1	2-17	0-1	0-2	2-16	0.00
Woodman	5-45	11.1	0-0	1-3	1-14	0-0	0-2	3-26	-14.67
Compton Place	5-51	9.8	1-8	1-10	1-10	1-1	1-6	0-16	**+24.00**
Atraf	5-64	7.8	0-6	2-14	2-9	0-2	0-12	1-21	-2.88
Night Shift	5-70	7.1	1-7	1-17	0-22	0-4	0-5	3-15	-43.63
Cadeaux Genereux	5-82	6.1	2-4	1-10	1-24	0-0	0-9	1-35	-56.00

CHAPTER FIVE

FORM ASSESSMENT

It still amazes me how many people think they can consistently win money by simply studying the cards in the racing pages of their daily newspapers. Don't get me wrong, the racing columnists in most of the top papers do a wonderful job and work very hard to provide as much information as possible for their readers. I speak from experience, even more so than when I wrote the original book five years ago, but racing journalists do have a problem.

Imagine that after hours of long and arduous study, a journalist uncovers what they believe to be a nailing good bet for that particular day. They write an utterly convincing piece which gives several sound reasons why this horse must have a great chance of winning and after having read it you are extremely tempted to get on. The trouble is that everyone who reads that piece is going to get the same message and if the horse should actually go and win, the profile of that writer will be raised so much more. String a few successes together and bung in a couple of long-priced winners and the world and his wife will all want to be on next time. The result? The best prices disappear and unless you're quick off the mark, the value train will have long departed by the time you place your bet.

Years ago when I practised the rather unhealthy habit of hanging around my local betting shop, there was a friend of mine who would habitually back the selections of well-known tipster in one of the trade papers (*The Sporting Life* was still around in those days), but he would make it sound as if the reasoning for picking a particular horse was all his. He would occasionally let slip that the newspaper tipster had selected it, which became obvious when I read the same column a bit later. My friend had almost quoted the column word for word, but it didn't stop him from walking about with a certain air of superiority if the horse won.

My friend had a certain problem with All-Weather racing though, because the tipsters in many of the daily newspapers also had a problem with All-Weather racing. These days most form guides will distinguish All-Weather form figures from those on turf by showing them in a bold font, but that's usually as far as it goes, and many of the ratings services these newspapers carried tended to treat all Flat form as though it were the same. There was many an occasion when a horse running on sand appeared to have a huge ratings advantage over the others, and on many occasions this was due to the fact that the horse had been rated on its turf form. The animal in question therefore appeared to be 'thrown in' and anyone following these ratings must have assumed the horse merely had to trot down to the start and canter back. Even these days, how often do you read that a certain horse is 'thrown in on its turf form and must take all the beating if handling the surface'. Unfortunately the word 'if' is vastly overused in racing.

Imagine seeing the following horse amongst the runners in a race at a hypothetical All-weather meeting.

Form	Name	Age/weight	Trainer	Jockey
010011	Quicksand	3-8-11	A Groom	S Journeyman

Let's assume that Quicksand has only run six times in his life, so his form figures represent his whole racing career. Has he got a chance in today's race? Obviously we can't really be sure, because we don't know the strength of the opposition and we don't know the race conditions, but what if his form was shown like this –

Form	Name	Age/weight	Trainer	Jockey
010011	Quicksand	3-8-11	A Groom	S Journeyman

As far as I'm concerned this horse has now become an automatic throw-out, but you can bet your life he will start at a shorter price than he should because of those three turf victories. You can forgive one modest performance on sand, especially at the first attempt, but I wouldn't want to put money on this horse suddenly translating his turf form on to sand. If he hasn't done so in three attempts so far, there is no reason why he should do it on the fourth.

The lesson here is simple, but it's one that a large number of people do not heed. I virtually discard form shown on turf when analysing an

All-Weather race and suggest you do the same. Of course horses do win on sand at the first time of asking, but no-one really knows how they will take to it, so there is an awful lot of guesswork involved.

If you like to use official handicap marks as a guide, you could always update your records on a daily basis for all horses that race on sand. For example, the results sections of the daily and weekly trade papers show the official mark the horse runs off in handicaps, so by keeping these details up to date you could end up with something like this –

Sorbiesharry 63_1 70_1 72_2 75_0 73_8 73_8

The smaller figure just to the right of each official mark shows where Sorbiesharry finished in that race. This example only shows his last six performances, but you can go back as far as you like and can be as detailed as you want (you could show the track, distance, date, etc). By noting the circumstances under which those previous performances were achieved, you can get a pretty good idea of how the horse will fare under future conditions and may also help show you where a horse's class barrier might lie. (Chapter Nine deals with the use of performance and speed ratings in more detail.)

The point I'm trying to make is that whatever form of ratings you use, make sure that only previous form shown on sand is included. An outing on turf only acts as a guide to the likely fitness of the horse in question and the following example shows how useful this type of approach can be.

On 8 May 1998, the feature race on Lingfield's mixed turf/All-Weather card was the Tote Handicap over one mile on the old Equitrack, a Class D event for four-year-olds and upwards rated 0 to 85. A field of 12 went to post and the 9/4 favourite was a horse called Sweet Wilhelmina, ridden by Frankie Dettori. According to my own speed ratings she was a contender, but the horse that interested me the most was a colt named Zimiri. The James Toller-trained four-year-old had run a total of six times before. He had finished unplaced on his two-year-old debut on turf at Kempton in September 1996, but his next start three months later was in a maiden over a mile on the Lingfield Equitrack, identical conditions to today's race. He managed to win that contest in a time which was just over four seconds faster than the second division of the same event and it earned Zimiri a huge speed figure from me.

He ran just four times the following year, all of them on turf, and his record read – sixth of six, ninth of nine, seventh of seven and twenty-second of twenty-two. In other words, he had failed to beat a single horse in his entire three-year-old campaign, and this Lingfield handicap was to be his first start at as a four-year-old.

To all intents and purposes, his form figures were

01/0000-

On the other hand, by stripping out the turf runs you were left with

1/

Anyone who used this method, especially if they compiled their own speed ratings or followed a set of established speed ratings, would have considered this horse to be an unbeaten All-Weather performer whose only previous effort under today's conditions had been out of this world judging by the clock. Those four desperate efforts in 1997 merely confirmed that Zimiri was alive and well as a three-year-old, and nothing more as far as his ability on sand was concerned.

The result? Zimiri came with a late run to pass Sweet Wilhelmina inside the last furlong and win by three-quarters of a length at odds of 33/1 (£53.70 on the Tote). Unfortunately, due to work commitments I was tied up all day and did not have a penny on.

I mentioned earlier how often form guides use performances on turf as the basis for selecting a certain horse when it makes its sand debut. Part of the reason for this I believe is that even these days some people regard switching a horse on to sand to be a step down in class, rather like dropping into a seller. However, as far as I can see if a horse runs in Class 4 company on turf and then appears at the same level on sand, he is facing exactly the same task in terms of the quality of the opposition, but with the added burden that he will likely be facing horses who have already proved themselves on the surface.

When an experienced horse is asked to race on sand for the first time, I am naturally cynical. If the same horse is all the rage in the form guides based on form shown on turf, then I become downright hostile! The old adage that you can't teach an old dog new tricks has never been more relevant and there have been several occasions when horses who could have carried the opposition on turf have completely flopped on sand.

One of the highest profile cases was that of Centre Stalls, who started 6/5 favourite for the Listed Wulfrun Stakes at Wolverhampton in December 1997. Centre Stalls had already won at Listed level on turf and been running against the very top milers that season. His best performance came at Royal Ascot when he chased home Allied Forces in the Group Two Queen Anne Stakes, and many assumed that the Wolverhampton event would be just a steering job for Richard Quinn. Unfortunately, the extended nine furlongs around two bends at Wolverhampton is about as different as you can possibly get to the straight mile at Ascot, and that's even without the vastly different racing surface! Centre Stalls had no previous experience of racing on sand and I'm afraid it showed. A brief effort half a mile out came to little and he also hung badly on the home bend, eventually coming home last of the seven runners. The official explanation was that Centre Stalls 'was unable to act on the surface' and that just about said it all.

The examples of Zimiri and Centre Stalls show how different turf and sand can be, but of course since then both Lingfield and Wolverhampton have taken the Polytrack route which has given the impression that horses are finding it easier to make the transition from turf to Polytrack than they did on other surfaces. Admittedly there are more horses winning on Polytrack at the first time of asking, but I would dispute that this is because they are finding the surface more akin to turf and are therefore able to show their best form. I believe it's because the Polytrack is such an accommodating surface that trainers like it and trust it. As a result they have been running their better horses on it rather than asking them to race on very firm or very soft ground on turf.

As I will suggest a bit later, classier horses are more able to transfer their ability between varying surfaces and I believe this is why we are seeing more horses taking to Polytrack straight away. It's because they have the class to do so, but I still prefer to rely on established form shown on sand rather than pure guesswork, and believe strongly that is the best way to go.

My rule of thumb is, unless those horses with previous experience on sand have conclusively proved themselves to be moderate, give form shown on sand priority over form shown on turf. Another thing to bear in mind is to watch out for horses that have shown a marked preference for certain conditions and only produce their best form when those conditions prevail.

For example, some horses are able to win over the five-furlong track at Lingfield or Wolverhampton, but can't do it at Southwell because they prefer Polytrack or are more effective racing around a bend. Others prefer the five furlongs at Southwell because they are resolute gallopers suited by running in a straight line.

Here are a couple of examples of horses that tend to show their best form under easily identifiable conditions.

Note – the details shown below are, from left to right: Date of race, Track, Distance in furlongs, Going (VF –Very Fast, FT – Fast, SD – Standard, SW – Slow, VS – Very Slow), Race description (the number shows the race class between 1 and 7, the letter is the race type (H –Handicap, C – Claimer, L – Limited or Classified stakes, S – Seller, N –Non-handicap or conditions race, M – Maiden, B – Banded race), Finishing position, Number of runners, Weight carried, Draw, Early pace description (L – Led Early, P – Prominent early, H – Held up off the pace), Speed rating.

TE QUIERO										
28 DEC 00	LING	12	FT	3H	8	12	8-1	7	H	100
19 OCT 02	WOLV	8.5	FT	6H	1	12	10-0	12	P	102
13 NOV 02	LING	8	SD	5H	11	12	9-11	3	L	82
07 DEC 02	WOLV	9.4	SD	5H	1	13	10-0	12	L	95
14 DEC 02	WOLV	9.4	SD	4H	1	7	9-3	7	L	101
13 JAN 03	WOLV	9.4	SW	4H	2	12	10-0	6	L	100
22 JAN 03	LING	10	SD	4H	14	14	9-13	11	L	64
08 MAR 03	WOLV	8.5	SW	2H	1	13	9-8	11	L	104
17 NOV 03	WOLV	8.5	SD	3H	5	13	9-12	6	P	100
03 DEC 03	SOUT	8	FT	3H	2	12	10-0	8	P	108
19 DEC 03	SOUT	12	SD	3H	3	8	10-0	3	L	107
31 DEC 03	WOLV	9.4	VS	3H	9	10	9-10	1	L	91
15 JAN 04	SOUT	7	FT	3H	9	16	10-0	15	H	97
24 JAN 04	LING	12	SD	3H	8	16	10-0	2	H	92
31 JAN 04	LING	10	SW	3H	11	13	9-4	2	L	82
20 FEB 04	WOLV	8.5	VS	3H	2	12	9-10	2	H	109
13 MAR04	WOLV	8.5	VS	2H	2	12	9-2	3	L	114
28 OCT 04	LING	7	SD	3H	11	13	9-4	6	H	101
20 NOV 04	LING	7	FT	3H	12	14	9-2	7	H	98
01 JAN 05	SOUT	8	SD	3H	3	12	9-7	11	P	113
20 JAN 05	SOUT	7	FT	3H	1	12	9-0	7	P	110
28 JAN 05	WOLV	8.6	SD	3N	7	8	9-11	1	P	91
10 FEB 05	SOUT	7	FT	3H	10	12	9-2	11	P	91
12 MAR 05	WOLV	7.1	SD	3N	5	7	9-0	7	H	95

We can see straight away that Te Quiero is a different horse on Fibresand, with an overall record of five wins and six placings from 15 starts on the surface. Compare that with his record on Equitrack/ Polytrack, no better than fifth in nine attempts.

Being able to see the horse's profile like this gives you invaluable information about its preferences. Even if you don't have the time to put a profile like this together yourself, many publications list a horse's form in this way or at least show the circumstances under which a horse has gained all of its victories. Te Quiero's requirements stick out like a sore thumb when shown in this way.

Here is another recent example.

PEAK PARK										
15 OCT 03	LING	16	SD	5H	11	13	7-13	14	P	88
01 SEP 04	LING	16	SD	6H	2	14	8-11	11	P	101
13 OCT 04	LING	16	SD	6H	2	14	8-13	6	H	100
06 NOV 04	WOLV	16.5	SD	6H	3	13	8-13	6	H	95
30 NOV 04	LING	16	SD	6H	6	13	10-9	13	H	89
14 DEC 04	SOUT	16	FT	6H	1	9	8-10	6	P	101
01 JAN 05	SOUT	16	SD	5H	3	12	8-8	10	H	98
22 JAN 05	LING	16	FT	5H	5	13	8-7	10	H	102
10 FEB 05	SOUT	16	FT	6H	1	9	9-2	7	H	102
24 FEB 05	SOUT	14	FT	5H	1	10	8-12	4	P	102
21 MAR 05	SOUT	16	SD	5H	1	9	9-1	3	P	103
21 MAY 05	LING	16	SD	3H	8	9	8-4	6	P	100

Although already placed a few times on Polytrack, Peak Park thrived after being switched to Fibresand, winning four times and finishing third from five outings on that surface during the winter of 2004/5.

One thing that I have noticed over the years is that specific requirements seem to be of more significance to horses lower down the scale. Admittedly Te Quiero is a useful performer on sand with a current official rating of 95, but having looked into the profiles of many horses of varying ability, I found that in general better horses were able to cope with a greater variety of circumstances than their modest counterparts.

As I mentioned earlier, the reason we are seeing more horses taking to Polytrack at the first time of asking is because classier types are attempting it and this is a case of where class tells. A few seasons back a very decent performer called Refuse To Lose showed how a talented horse could maintain a high level of form on several different surfaces.

Not only did he win the Royal Hunt Cup over the straight mile at Royal Ascot, he also won the Listed Wulfrun Stakes on Fibresand at Wolverhampton and was a very effective performer on Equitrack too.

Here are a couple of more recent examples of horses that are able to show high-class form on different All-Weather surfaces.

VORTEX											
14 DEC 02	WOLV	7	SD	4M	8	10	9-0	4	P	81
28 DEC02	LING	7	SW	4M	1	15	9-0	5	H	97
19 JUL 03	WOLV	7	SD	5L	1	7	8-12	1	P	103
19 JAN 04	WOLV	8.5	SD	4H	1	13	9-9	12	H	105
31 JAN04	LING	8	SW	4H	1	12	9-11	4	P	98
14 FEB 04	WOLV	8.5	VS	4H	1	12	9-7	1	L	104
23 FEB 04	WOLV	8.5	VS	4H	1	7	9-12	6	H	101
13 MAR 04	WOLV	8.5	VS	2H	1	12	8-12	13	H	114
20 MAR 04	LING	10	SD	1N	12	14	8-12	10	H	97
12 MAR 05	WOLV	8.6	SD	2H	2	13	9-10	11	H	110
09 APR 05	LING	7	FT	4N	1	6	9-12	2	P	111
09 JUL 05	LING	8	SD	G3	3	12	9-2	11	H	111

Te Quiero's stable-companion Vortex is a 110-rated performer and has shown very high-class form on every domestic sand surface in the last few years. Just for good measure, he has also won two Listed races on sand in Scandinavia and is a Group Three winner on turf too.

Here is one more example.

FALL IN LINE											
08 AUG 03	WOLV	9.4	SD	4M	3	10	9-0	6	H	85
26 SEP 03	SOUT	12	VS	4M	3	16	8-13	3	L	101
26 JAN 04	WOLV	12	SW	5H	1	12	9-0	4	L	116
29 JAN 04	SOUT	12	SD	5H	1	7	9-2	5	P	108
31 JAN 04	LING	13	SW	5L	1	11	9-6	2	L	102
03 FEB 04	SOUT	11	SD	5H	1	12	9-8	11	P	111
04 FEB 04	LING	12	SD	4H	1	15	8-11	13	P	107
07 FEB 04	LING	10	FT	5L	1	13	9-6	6	L	104

Sir Mark Prescott's Fall In Line achieved an amazing feat at the start of 2004, winning six times on sand within the space of 13 days. Three victories came on Polytrack and three on Fibresand over distances ranging from ten to 13 furlongs. Notice also that he usually had to do it the hard way, either from the front or after racing close to the pace.

So in order to summarise, the better the horse the more likely he or she is to translate their ability between different surfaces, whereas horses of more modest ability are more likely to show their best form under specific conditions.

Regional Racing
I'm not a great fan of Regional Racing, usually referred to as Banded (or bandit) racing, but that's no reason not to mention it.

Banded racing is not the preserve of the All-Weather tracks, but there are a large number of fixtures that fall in the winter months. A few years ago I remember reading a book on betting which stated that 'unreliable horses provide unreliable form', but unlike some pieces of accepted wisdom, this statement has an element of truth about it, and I'm afraid you can't get much more unreliable than many of the horses that run in banded races.

When I refer to banded racing I am not including sellers, claimers or maidens run at Regional meetings, as these races are not restricted to very lowly rated horses. It has sometimes been a source of great amusement that the seller at a Regional meeting is the classiest race on the card, and often it happens to be true.

As far as I can see, horses that run in banded contests do so because:

1) They are completely devoid of any ability.

2) They have seen better days, are in the autumn of their careers and are very much on the decline.

3) They possess some talent but have lost their way, either because they have lost their confidence or because of a physical problem.

4) For one reason or another, they have not yet had the chance to show their true ability.

Those in the top two categories are easy to spot and just as easy to dismiss. Those in the top group continue to get soundly beaten even after they have been dropped into banded class, whilst those in the second group usually have an awful lot of miles on the clock and are a light of former days. Admittedly the 14-year-old Redoubtable did pop up at

Southwell at odds of 28/1 in January 2005, but it was very much a rarity and you can afford to miss occasions like that.

Those in the other two categories are much more interesting. As a rule they should have demonstrated some signs of ability before dropping to banded company, but they should be lightly raced and preferably no older than four years of age. Also, if the horse in question has moved to a trainer who has a decent track record with other people's cast-offs, on sand in general but in banded company in particular, then that is a major positive.

To name but a few, Tony Carroll, David Flood, Mark Brisbourne and Ron Harris are the sort of names I look for if I'm having a bet in these types of races. There are other very capable trainers of course, but I have noticed that these gentlemen are particularly gifted at getting the best out of the horses they receive from elsewhere. It may be because they have more time and patience than a so-called major stable in order to sort the horse out, or perhaps by curing any physical cause for the individual not showing its best.

The betting market is of course a very useful barometer in racing, but it does seem to be very true of banded racing. Admittedly the on-course market at Regional All-Weather meetings is very weak (you only have to turn up to a midweek fixture in the winter to see why), but there have been quite a few occasions when all you had to do was spot the gamble to find the winner of a banded race. Just witness the market support for Barney Curley's pair Ndola and Dafa before they won their respective contests. It also seems that when a horse is strongly fancied the price can shorten very quickly indeed, so if you have to have a bet in a race like this, watch the market and if there is a positive move for your selection get on quick before the price collapses.

Another thing I have noticed is that once a horse has its confidence restored by winning in banded company, they can often run up a sequence. Quite a few did this during the winter of 2004/5, such as Attorney who won four in a row at the start of 2005 before stepping up in grade and winning one more on sand and three on turf in the spring. Tee Jay Kassidy completed a four-timer at the end of 2004, whilst Set Alight did the same thing early in 2005. Fraternity won five times from six starts early in 2005 and in each of these cases it all started with a return to winning form in banded company.

Although some of these horses were able to maintain their resurgence in higher grade, it's probably best not to invest too much money on a banded-class winner until they demonstrate that they can cope with a rise in grade. It seemed to me that the majority of banded-stakes winners couldn't hack it in better company, but I had no statistics to prove it, until now.

I wrote a computer programme to work out how well horses did in higher-class races after they had won a banded contest, and the results were very interesting. Between 1 January 2004 and 31 July 2005, after winning for the first time at that level, banded-stakes winners subsequently ran a total of 999 times in higher-class contests on sand and won 105 of them, or 11%. Contrast that with how well banded-stakes winners did when returning at the same level subsequently.

During the same period, banded-stakes winners ran in a total of 284 races of the same type on sand afterwards, winning 121 of them (43%). Clearly, banded-stakes winners have a great record when they reappear in the same grade, though that is entirely in the hands of the Handicapper.

Finally, if you want to see an example of a horse with an obvious class barrier outside of banded company, then look at the following sand profile of a horse called Dial Square.

DIAL SQUARE										
10 NOV 03	WOLV	6	SD	4M	11	13	9-0	8	H	72
14 JAN 04	WOLV	7	SD	7M	9	11	8-6	5	P	74
03 FEB 04	LING	8	SW	7B	1	11	8-2	11	P	90
14 MAR 04	LING	7	SW	6H	3	15	7-13	10	P	98
29 MAR 04	LING	7	SD	7B	2	15	8-6	10	P	95
06 APR 04	LING	8	SD	7B	3	12	8-6	8	P	94
19 APR 04	LING	8	SD	7B	1	6	9-0	1	H	97
27 APR 04	LING	8	SD	7B	1	5	9-6	2	H	100
29 APR 04	LING	10	SW	7B	1	4	9-6	3	H	84
03 NOV 04	WOLV	8.6	SW	6L	10	12	9-2	5	H	92
06 NOV 04	WOLV	8.6	SD	6H	9	13	8-13	6	H	88
15 NOV 04	WOLV	12.2	FT	7B	12	12	9-2	10	H	77
22 JAN 05	LING	10	FT	6L	11	14	9-0	1	H	91
02 FEB 05	LING	10	SD	7B	1	13	9-2	4	H	101
14 FEB 05	LING	10	SD	7B	6	13	8-12	2	H	98
21 FEB 05	LING	10	FT	6H	4	14	8-4	11	H	101
28 FEB 05	LING	8	SD	7B	2	11	9-5	10	P	95
08 MAR 05	SOUT	7	SD	6L	5	14	9-3	10	H	97
21 MAR 05	LING	10	SD	6H	10	14	8-7	10	P	95
23 MAR 05	LING	8	SD	6H	3	12	9-1	4	H	94

31 MAR 05	LING	10	FT	7B	7	14	9-7	4	H	101
05 APR 05	SOUT	8	SD	7B	7	10	8-13	6	H	88
28 APR 05	LING	10	VF	7B	6	14	9-3	9	H	99
06 JUL 05	LING	10	SW	6S	6	12	9-12	8	H	92
16 JUL 05	LING	10	VS	6S	13	14	9-11	6	P	75

CHAPTER SIX

EARLY PACE

If there is one impact I would really like this book to make, then it's to provide information and guidance to the reader without them having to learn the hard way, i.e. by losing money. When I wrote the original book five years ago, I did so having digested as much information as I could from those books on handicapping and form assessment available at the time, many of them by American authors, though not all. I thought that the advice and information I had taken in would help me avoid the pitfalls that tend to haunt the novice and suck away his or her betting bank without mercy.

You will have no doubt noticed my liking for speed ratings and it was on sand in those early years (covered in Chapter One) that I got used to *compiling* them for my own benefit and *using* them for the same reason. Unfortunately compiling speed ratings and using them to advantage is not the same thing. I became quite proficient at calculating them, but it took an awful lot longer before I used them properly and there was one area that cost me dear before the penny finally dropped.

Quite often I would compile my speed ratings for an All-Weather card and on many occasions I would find what looked to me to be a standout bet. Usually the horse involved had speed figures that were generally higher than its opponents, the trip would be fine, the surface would be ok and all seemed well with the world. I would then place my bet, usually a decent one, and watch in complete horror as the animal got stuffed. I could never quite understand why and usually I blamed the jockey for an inept ride, or worse. I even put it down to the fact that I was dealing with flesh and blood (the old 'they aren't machines' cliché). If only I had thought about it deeper, the reason for my distressing experiences would have been staring me in the face.

In many cases the horse I liked was a front-runner who came off the bridle much earlier than I had expected before falling in a heap. It was then that I realised that the reason the horse had flopped was because he had probably earned his superior figures when able to dominate from the front but, when taken on too early, the physical tiredness combined with the mental tiredness of trying to ward off the attentions of another horse, before the run to the line had started, had compromised his chance. I looked into the whole subject further and found out that in many instances the scenario I have just described had indeed occurred. I also found out that in some other cases the horse's draw had made it very difficult to gain an early lead, and that had contributed to its downfall. In some other instances a change in trip had necessitated a change of tactics and a confirmed front-runner was being asked to alter its running style. Usually it didn't work.

The question was, how was I going to find out whether my selection's chance was going to be helped or hindered by the way the race was going to be run? I already had a database of All-Weather results that contained several bits of information about each horse's past performances, but I didn't have any information on the early position the individual took during each contest. Had they led early or were they held up? I needed a way of seeing at a glance a horse's running style in its past performances, so that I could use that information when the horse ran again.

What I eventually came up with was a single-letter description, or early pace symbol, which would show the position the horse took in the early stages of the race. I use just three letters, 'L' means 'led early', which is within the first furlong of any race, 'P' means 'prominent early' and 'H' is for 'held up', but also covers everything else. I decide which letter to apply by looking at the comments-in-running that appear in the results sections of the daily and weekly racing papers, or in the formbook. For example, a comment that says 'led early' would get an 'L', and so would 'made all'. On the other hand, 'in touch' or 'close up' would get a 'P', whilst 'held up' or 'outpaced' would get an 'H'.

This may seem rather crude and of course I could use other letters to be even more specific about the early position a horse might take, but I don't for two very good reasons. Firstly, by only using three letters their meanings are clear to me and using many more symbols could get very confusing. Secondly and most importantly, I'm really only interested in those horses who like to lead or take a prominent position. By identifying how many horses like to lead early, I can predict with some accuracy whether the pace is likely to be strong or if one horse is likely to have a solo out in front (and increase his chances of making all in the process). It will also tell me whether my particular selection will be suited by the way the race is likely to be run.

By using this method along with the draw and front-runners' statistics in the previous chapters, I have a formidable weapon in my armoury. Early pace is still a big asset in All-Weather racing despite the Lingfield Polytrack giving hold-up horses more of a chance. At Southwell especially, horses that need to be produced late find it difficult to accelerate on the surface and also have the added burden of having to face the kickback in big fields.

Of course there were many occasions when I really fancied a hold-up performer because of its superior speed figures, only to see the horse sunk by a lack of early pace, which led to a sprint finish and a questionable result. This happened with increased regularity in the first few years of the Lingfield Polytrack in races beyond ten furlongs. No wonder I began to hate the place.

Having flushed too much money down the toilet in this fashion, I decided that identifying early pace would become an even more important part of my form study. It had been important before, but now it would cause me to turn my ratings on their head (something that would have been unthinkable five years ago) if the shape of the race was not going to suit my original selection. This meant that sometimes I had to sit on my hands and resist backing a horse if I was sure its chance was going to be compromised, even if it was way ahead of the opposition on my speed figures. Usually that proved the right thing to do.

I realise that keeping the sort of pace records I have described isn't possible for everyone, but that isn't to say it's impossible to find a horse's running style for an upcoming race. The *Raceform Update* cards now carry a pace symbol for each horse in its cards covering racing between Wednesday and Sunday. These symbols, based on each horse's previous running style, are similar to my own and at least give you an idea of the position the horse will take early. Failing that, the form section of the *Racing Post* gives a comment-in-running for each horse in its recent starts and glancing at those will give you invaluable information on their running styles. Whichever method you use, the results can be dramatic.

Just to give an example of how valuable this information can be, and to summarise everything that has been mentioned in this chapter so far, here is an example of a real race when everything came together very nicely. The race concerned was the Moorcroft Racehorse Welfare Centre Banded Stakes, run at Wolverhampton on Monday 16 May 2005. (In order to save space, only each runner's previous sand form in 2005 is shown).

4-30 MOORCROFT RACEHORSE WELFARE CENTRE BANDED STAKES (0-40) (7) 3YO+
6 furlongs Par = 97 11 runners

1 1 BAYTOWN FLYER			8-11			P S MCENTEE			B REILLY(3)		
04 JAN 05	WOLV	5.1	SD	7B	5	13	8-10	8	P	93
24 JAN 05	WOLV	6	SD	7B	9	12	8-7	7	L	91
02 FEB 05	LING	7	SD	7B	3	13	8-11	13	L	97
22 FEB 05	LING	6	SD	6C	8	12	8-0	1	L	89
28 FEB 05	LING	6	SD	7B	4	11	9-0	9	L	95
15 MAR 05	SOUT	6	SD	7B	7	9	8-9	4	L	82
05 APR 05	SOUT	6	SD	7B	10	11	8-4	5	L	76
28 APR 05	LING	6	VF	7B	3	11	9-4	4	P	93

2 6 COMIC TALES			8-11			M MULLINEAUX			A MCCARTHY		
07 FEB 05	WOLV	6	FT	7B	4	12	8-2	7	H	88
13 MAR 05	WOLV	6	FT	7B	3	13	8-12	8	H	91
19 MAR 05	WOLV	8.6	FT	7B	13	13	9-2	11	H	80
15 APR 05	WOLV	6	SD	7B	4	13	9-0	9	H	89
25 APR 05	SOUT	5	SD	7B	6	10	9-0	3	H	86

3 7 DRUMACOLE ARTIST			8-11(B)			W A MURPHY			F NORTON		

4 11 EAGER ANGEL			8-11(TB)			R F MARVIN			L FLETCHER		
20 JAN 05	SOUT	6	FT	6L	10	10	8-8	4	H	79
27 FEB 05	WOLV	7.1	FT	7B	10	11	8-12	2	H	75

5 9 HEATHYARDSBLESSING			8-11(V)			R HOLLINSHEAD			DALE GIBSON		
04 JAN 05	WOLV	7.1	SD	7B	9	12	8-11	3	H	83
12 JAN 05	WOLV	5.1	SD	6C	4	9	8-0	4	P	82
01 FEB 05	SOUT	5	FT	7B	13	13	8-11	13	P	70
14 FEB 05	LING	6	SD	7B	8	11	9-0	8	P	91
21 FEB 05	WOLV	5.1	FT	7B	4	12	8-12	8	H	93
13 MAR 05	WOLV	6	FT	7B	2	13	8-12	11	H	91
26 MAR 05	WOLV	6	FT	7B	4	12	9-0	8	H	94
15 APR 05	WOLV	6	SD	7B	3	13	9-0	1	P	91

6 2 JODONSTAY			8-11			D SHAW			B SWARBRICK(5)		
01 FEB 05	SOUT	6	FT	7C	10	13	8-4	6	P	75
15 FEB 05	SOUT	7	FT	7C	10	10	9-4	1	P	48

7 3 JUNIPER BANKS				8-11(V)		MISS A STOKELL		ANN STOKELL		
06 JAN 05	WOLV	5.1	SD	4M	7	12	9-0	2	P	88
27 JAN 05	SOUT	6	FT	4M	6	11	9-9	7	P	85
08 FEB 05	SOUT	6	SD	4M	13	13	9-10	6	H	57
21 FEB 05	WOLV	5.1	FT	7B	9	12	8-12	12	H	88
24 FEB 05	SOUT	5	SD	4M	9	11	9-11	3	H	81

8 5 OFF HIRE				8-11(V)		C SMITH		R FITZPATRICK		
15 FEB 05	SOUT	6	FT	7B	8	14	8-13	7	P	83
22 FEB 05	SOUT	5	SW	7B	6	13	9-2	2	P	86
21 MAR 05	SOUT	6	SD	6C	5	10	9-1	3	P	84
05 APR 05	SOUT	5	VF	7B	9	13	9-0	3	P	85

9 4 CADOGEN SQUARE				8-2		D W CHAPMAN		J MACKAY		
03 JAN 05	SOUT	6	SD	6H	11	11	8-5	11	H	51
24 FEB 05	SOUT	5	SD	4M	8	11	8-6	2	P	82

10 8 ROBURY				8-2		E J ALSTON		D ALLAN		

11 10 STARLIGHT RIVER				8-2		J PARKES		C CATLIN		
03 JAN 05	SOUT	6	SD	6H	4	11	8-13	9	P	87
28 JAN 05	WOLV	7.1	SD	6H	12	12	8-10	7	P	78
12 MAR 05	SOUT	6	FT	7B	12	14	8-2	12	P	69
05 APR 05	SOUT	5	VF	7B	11	13	8-5	6	H	83
21 APR 05	SOUT	8	FT	6H	4	7	8-3	6	P	88

DRAW AND FRONT-RUNNER STATISTICS FOR 6 FURLONGS DURING PAST 12 MONTHS

Draw Pos	Winners	%
Low	41	48
Middle	27	31
High	17	20

Draw No	Runners	Winners	%
1	84	17	20
2	84	5	6
3	83	10	12
4	82	14	17
5	81	11	14
6	78	5	6
7	82	2	2
8	78	5	6
9	78	6	8
10	74	2	3
11	69	2	3

Front-runners Impact Value = 1.6
Prominent Horses Impact Value = 0.9
Hold Up Horses Impact Value = 0.9

Date	Going	Draw	Runners	Early Pos	Winners Name
WINNING DRAW POSITIONS OF LAST 20 RACES OVER 6 FURLONGS					
19 FEB 05	FT	5	12	L	STARGEM
21 FEB 05	FT	8	10	H	JUSTENJOY YOURSELF
27 FEB 05	FT	1	13	L	FRATERNITY
28 FEB 05	SD	5	7	H	PERSEA
04 MAR 05	SD	1	10	H	MARKO JADEO
04 MAR 05	SD	1	9	P	KINGSMAITE
07 MAR 05	SD	1	13	P	RASSEEM
07 MAR 05	SD	3	4	P	STORYVILLE
12 MAR 05	SD	4	10	H	KATIYPOUR
13 MAR 05	FT	12	13	H	ORCHESTRATION
13 MAR 05	FT	12	13	P	AL AWWAM
16 MAR 05	SD	1	13	H	MOLLZAM
19 MAR 05	FT	4	13	L	FLYING EDGE
26 MAR 05	FT	1	12	L	CLEVELAND WAY
02 APR 05	FT	7	9	P	GILDED COVE
15 APR 05	SD	4	13	P	GRAND VIEW
16 APR 05	FT	3	13	L	GONE'N'DUNNETT
18 APR 05	FT	10	12	P	DAVID'S SYMPHONY
23 APR 05	FT	12	13	L	COLOURFUL ERA
25 APR 05	VF	1	12	P	LADY VEE

As soon as I started to look at this race it almost seemed too good to be true. Baytown Flyer looked to be a case of 'Christmas come early'. Admittedly, she didn't have much form at Wolverhampton to her name, but that is where the negatives ended. The trip wasn't a problem and she was the only one in the field whose speed figures showed she was capable of winning in this grade. She was drawn in stall one, which the draw statistics showed was the most successful berth over this trip in the previous year, and front-runners (which she certainly was according to my pace symbols) had an impact value of 1.6. Even so, all of this would have meant little had there been another habitual front-runner in the field, but there wasn't. It seemed inconceivable that Baytown Flyer wasn't going to break quickly from stall one and make every yard. The only surprise to me was that she was allowed to start at 9/4 against when I was convinced she was going to be odds-on. Sometimes you just have to close your eyes and dive in, and that is exactly what I did, striking a bet that was certainly near the upper end of my emotional limit.

Once the stalls opened the result was never in doubt. Despite the best efforts of Cadogen Square to hang on to her tail, Baytown Flyer made every yard to beat her by a length and a half with the others upwards of five lengths away.

Every race on sand requires that the prospective shape of the contest is analysed in the same way and although this particular scenario only occurs every so often, there will be other occasions when the boot is on the other foot and a forecast favourite is worth laying or taking on with another selection(s) because he or she is not going to have the race run to suit.

CHAPTER SEVEN

TRACK CONDITION

I said earlier that the word 'if' was overused within the context of All-Weather racing with regard to whether a horse would click on sand at the first time of asking. Another overused word in All-Weather racing is 'Standard' when used to describe the official going. The problem is that there is no real method as far as I'm aware which will accurately describe the state of the track before the meeting has taken place. Unlike on turf, you can't go around and thrust a walking stick into the sand to see how far it goes in and base the official going report on that. So, unless some unique conditions are prevalent such as a monsoon of biblical proportions, the going will usually be reported as Standard, but just what exactly does 'Standard' mean?

When the first edition of this book was published, there were three official going descriptions which could be used for an All-Weather meeting, namely 'Fast', 'Standard' and 'Slow', but two more have been added since then to cover the areas between the three original descriptions. We now have 'Standard to Fast' and 'Standard to Slow' which is certainly an improvement, but just exactly how accurate are these official going descriptions? I have to say at this point that the Clerks Of The Course involved do a wonderful job in what is a very difficult area and they do have to provide a description of the going with the information available to them *before the meeting starts*. Of course they will know all about the preparation of the track beforehand and how the track has been rolled or harrowed, and from that they can make a prediction of how the track *might* ride, but in my opinion they are on a hiding to nothing.

As I stated five years ago, unlike Firm or Soft ground on turf, the going descriptions on sand tracks do not describe the physical effect the horse feels through its legs when galloping on the surface. Rather they describe the likely effect on race times at the meeting, and anyone with an interest in greyhound racing will be familiar with this concept. I use race times a great deal with regard to All-Weather racing and one of the things I use them for is to assess the state of the track *after the meeting has taken place* and calculate my own interpretation as to the true state of the ground. The results are a real eye-opener, as you can see for meetings held between 1 January and 15 June 2005. How many of these meetings had the official going described as Standard?

Lingfield			
04 JAN 05	−6	Fast	6.5
05 JAN 05	−4	Fast	5.4
08 JAN 05	−3	Standard	5.8
12 JAN 05	−4	Fast	3.2
13 JAN 05	−4	Fast	3.6
15 JAN 05	−3	Standard	2.5
19 JAN 05	−5	Fast	4.6
22 JAN 05	−8	Fast	3.1
26 JAN 05	−12	Very Fast	3.1
29 JAN 05	−5	Fast	4.1
01 FEB 05	−5	Fast	5.4
02 FEB 05	−3	Standard	3.0
05 FEB 05	+3	Standard	3.5
08 FEB 05	−1	Standard	5.1
09 FEB 05	−5	Fast	3.6
12 FEB 05	−1	Standard	3.6
14 FEB 05	−3	Standard	3.8
16 FEB 05	−4	Fast	4.0
21 FEB 05	+3	Standard	3.8
22 FEB 05	−2	Standard	2.5
23 FEB 05	−5	Fast	2.1
26 FEB 05	−2	Standard	6.4
28 FEB 05	−3	Standard	1.0
01 MAR 05	−5	Fast	4.1
03 MAR 05	+3	Standard	3.6
07 MAR 05	−1	Standard	4.5
18 MAR 05	−1	Standard	3.6
19 MAR 05	−1	Standard	5.8
21 MAR 05	0	Standard	3.3
22 MAR 05	−2	Standard	4.5
23 MAR 05	−2	Standard	2.0
31 MAR 05	−4	Fast	2.3
01 APR 05	−3	Standard	3.2
06 APR 05	0	Standard	4.5
08 APR 05	+1	Standard	6.8
09 APR 05	−6	Fast	6.2
11 APR 05	−1	Standard	5.1
20 APR 05	−6	Fast	4.0
28 APR 05	−10	Very Fast	1.7
17 MAY 05	+3	Standard	4.7

Southwell

01 JAN 05	0	Standard	5.2
02 JAN 05	−4	Fast	3.0
03 JAN 05	−1	Standard	6.0
05 JAN 05	−2	Standard	4.0
11 JAN 05	+5	Slow	3.0
13 JAN 05	−4	Fast	3.8
18 JAN 05	+3	Standard	4.4
20 JAN 05	−7	Fast	3.9
25 JAN 05	−8	Fast	5.0
27 JAN 05	−4	Fast	4.0
01 FEB 05	−8	Fast	6.0
03 FEB 05	−3	Standard	3.9
07 FEB 05	0	Standard	3.4
08 FEB 05	−3	Standard	3.8
10 FEB 05	−4	Fast	4.4
15 FEB 05	−9	Fast	6.7
17 FEB 05	−7	Fast	4.5
22 FEB 05	+3	Standard	4.2
24 FEB 05	−9	Fast	4.3
26 FEB 05	−8	Fast	5.9
02 MAR 05	−3	Standard	5.0
08 MAR 05	−1	Standard	3.6
12 MAR 05	−4	Fast	4.2
15 MAR 05	0	Standard	3.4
17 MAR 05	−2	Standard	3.0
21 MAR 05	−3	Standard	5.0
04 APR 05	−3	Standard	5.0
05 APR 05	−3	Standard	3.0
08 APR 05	−6	Fast	5.3
21 APR 05	−7	Fast	3.7
25 APR 05	−6	Fast	5.3
26 APR 05	−7	Fast	4.3
28 APR 05	−10	Very Fast	5.0
09 MAY 05	−9	Fast	3.4
18 MAY 05	−7	Fast	2.6

Wolverhampton

04 JAN 05	+1	Standard	3.2
06 JAN 05	+2	Standard	4.9
07 JAN 05	+9	Slow	2.5
10 JAN 05	−2	Standard	4.3
12 JAN 05	0	Standard	4.1
14 JAN 05	+2	Standard	3.0
17 JAN 05	0	Standard	4.7
21 JAN 05	−3	Standard	3.1
24 JAN 05	+3	Standard	1.7
28 JAN 05	0	Standard	2.5
31 JAN 05	−3	Standard	3.3
04 FEB 05	−2	Standard	1.0
06 FEB 05	-3	Standard	6.7
07 FEB 05	−6	Fast	1.0

11 FEB 05	−1	Standard	3.5
12 FEB 05	−6	Fast	5.5
14 FEB 05	−4	Fast	3.6
18 FEB 05	-4	Fast	3.6
19 FEB 05	−5	Fast	6.4
21 FEB 05	−7	Fast	3.2
25 FEB 05	−4	Fast	2.6
27 FEB 05	−6	Fast	3.8
28 FEB 05	0	Standard	4.1
04 MAR 05	0	Standard	4.3
07 MAR 05	0	Standard	5.3
12 MAR 05	−3	Standard	3.0
13 MAR 05	−5	Fast	2.3
16 MAR 05	0	Standard	3.1
19 MAR 05	-4	Fast	6.0
24 MAR 05	−3	Standard	3.1
26 MAR 05	−4	Fast	5.2
02 APR 05	-4	Fast	4.7
04 APR 05	-7	Fast	7.3
15 APR 05	−3	Standard	2.3
16 APR 05	−5	Fast	4.5
18 APR 05	−5	Fast	4.3
22 APR 05	−1	Standard	6.0
23 APR 05	−4	Fast	5.3
25 APR 05	−10	Very Fast	4.5
09 MAY 05	−7	Fast	4.7
16 MAY 05	−8	Fast	6.2
27 MAY 05	−3	Standard	2.3
01 JUN 05	−7	Fast	2.3
03 JUN 05	−5	Fast	4.0
09 JUN 05	−1	Standard	6.6
10 JUN 05	−3	Standard	7.5
16 JUN 05	−3	Standard	3.8

Note – Lingfield and Southwell also stage Flat racing on turf, so in the above lists only meetings that included at least four races on sand are shown. The figure after the date of each meeting is the number of lengths per mile the ground was either speeding the horses up or slowing them down. For example, a figure of −2 would mean that the ground was enabling the horses to run on average two lengths per mile faster than if the ground was perfectly Standard, whilst a figure of +10 means the track was slowing them down by ten lengths for every mile they ran. The final figure in each row is a pace figure. It shows how much front-runners were suited by the track. This figure is on a scale of 1 to 10, so a pace figure of 10 would mean that every race on the card was won by a horse that led early, whereas a figure of 1 would mean that all the winners came from off the pace.

Even this information requires a little bit of interpretation, For one thing, Standard going at Lingfield means Standard for the Lingfield Polytrack, but Standard going at Southwell means Standard for the Southwell Fibresand. The two Polytrack surfaces are different enough to mean that just because a horse has performed well on a Standard surface at one track does not mean it will do the same on another. Polytrack is a much faster surface than Fibresand, so in theory a Fast racing surface at Southwell would equate to a Standard surface at Lingfield. That is the theory, though I'm not quite so rigid in applying that rule. One rule I do tend to use however, is that if a horse has won over a certain trip on a 'Fast' surface at Lingfield, I do not conclude that it truly stays that particular distance until it has won or run very close on a slower surface.

The elements play their part in the condition of the track of course, but the effect is a little different to that on turf. If the heavens open and there is sufficient rain, grass tracks become ever softer, everyone understands that. On sand however, the effect is a little less predictable. When the rains come down in sufficient quantity, the All-Weather surfaces begin to look like the muddy entrance to a farmyard, but what happens to the track as far as the horses are concerned? The answer is, it is impossible to say until one or two races have been run on the surface. In many cases, the sand appears to become 'clingy' and have the same effect as muddy ground on turf. As a result, the race times become slower and any horses with stamina doubts are soon exposed. Occasionally, the surface seems to get quicker which seems illogical until you imagine a similar scenario on a beach. Where the sand remains dry and powdery it takes real effort to run through it, but where the tide comes in the sand is flattened and the surface becomes firmer, giving a truer footing and making it easier to run fast.

As I rule however, I don't assume that the surface has been affected in any way until I see evidence. I'm always on the lookout for any changes in the predictability of the track, even if the weather has been calm. Track maintenance takes place all the time, sometimes between races, and this can occasionally affect how the surface rides. So the message is, look to see if horses are being helped or hindered by racing on a certain part of the track or if there is an unusual bias towards or away from front-runners. Also keep your eyes and ears open for any information that may be forthcoming about track maintenance. To illustrate what I mean, here is a true story.

On 6 January 1999, I went to Wolverhampton (when they were still racing on Fibresand) and to say it was one of the wettest days I have ever witnessed would be an understatement. The rain was persistent and it never let up at any stage. There was so much rain in fact that the meeting was in danger of being abandoned. Puddles were starting to appear on the track and before the meeting was due to get under way, a posse of stewards, jockeys, trainers, officials, groundstaff, press and the like went out on to the track to examine the Fibresand. After what seemed like a long period of time, the powers that be decided to run the first race and see what happened, and then take another look afterwards. The public address also announced that 'power harrowing' would take place on the track before the first race and then between subsequent races if the meeting lasted that long. Power harrowing is the really heavy-duty stuff, the Fibresand being probed further down than would normally be the case and the surface water being dispersed. After the harrowing had been done, I noticed that the track looked much darker than it normally did. It was a very grey day, but there was no doubt that the surface was looking different. I wondered at that stage if it would also ride differently.

There was only one way to find out, so I waited patiently for the first race, the first division of a six-furlong amateur riders' handicap. Almost 20 minutes after the advertised off time, the race finally took place and was won by the 25/1 shot Another Nightmare, who made all, whilst the 11/10 favourite Theatre Magic started slowly and could never quite make up the ground, eventually finishing third. It didn't quite strike me at the time, mainly because I was licking my wounds after backing the favourite, but what I was seeing was the effect of the track maintenance.

The second race was the second division of the amateur riders' event. I managed to back the winner, the 2/1 favourite Baptismal Rock who, although not quite making all the running, was in the front rank from the start and was in front with over two furlongs left to run.

The third race, division one of the nine-furlong seller, was won by 9/2 shot Roffey Spinney, who again made all. I had not backed him and it was only at that point that the penny finally dropped.

As I saw it, nothing was able to come from off the pace under these conditions and, what was more, horses that stayed on the inside rail (unlike at most meetings) and raced close to the pace, or even made the running, had a big advantage on this day. I took a deep breath and decided to review my plan of attack for the rest of the meeting. There were five races left on the card, so there was still plenty of time to use this newly acquired knowledge.

The fourth race on the card was an all-age maiden over the extended mile and the Evens favourite was the Lord Huntingdon-trained Violet. I fancied her strongly as she did have the best form and also had my top speed figure, but she undoubtedly helped her chances in this race by racing close to the pace before taking it up with over three furlongs left to run. She extended the lead to over seven lengths on reaching the line to give her trainer the last domestic winner of his career.

The winner of the fifth race, Baron de Pichon, somewhat bucked the trend by being held up off the pace, but there were only seven runners and in truth he was never too far off the lead. Needless to say I didn't back him. However, it is worth noting that, rather like those that run well from a poor draw, any horse that can overcome unfavourable conditions and still win is probably better than the bare form would suggest. Baron de Pichon confirmed that philosophy by going on to win four of his next five starts.

Failed To Hit made all to win the mile-and-a-half handicap at 4/1. I didn't back him, but had considered him to be the main danger to my selection Alsahib, who finished fourth.

However, the day finished off with a flourish as I backed the last two winners, partly because they had competitive speed figures, but mainly because they both liked to race close to the pace and if they did the same today, they were going to help their winning chances no end. Fortunately they both adopted their normal running styles, Areish leading over two furlongs out before going on to win the second division of the seller at 4/1, and Trojan Girl leading at halfway before going on to win the closing five-furlong handicap by an easy three lengths at 9/4.

I congratulated myself on having used my eyes and ears to pick up the information that was available to me, and having the courage to change my approach once the meeting was under way. In reality you probably won't find it necessary to do it that often, but unusual circumstances do occur from time to time and you should be prepared to review your bets for the rest of the meeting should the need arise.

A rather more recent example of when spotting a pace bias early resulted in tasty profits occurred on 10 June 2005. Although I wasn't at the Wolverhampton meeting in person, I did watch with great interest from the office and was to eventually win a very tidy sum.

If you look at my going details earlier in this chapter, you will notice that the pace figure for this particular meeting was 7.5, one of the highest I have ever come across. Fortunately, I spotted what was happening with regards to the track during the meeting, therefore early enough to capitalise on it.

The first race on the card, an amateur riders' seller, was won by the 9/2 shot Explosive Fox, who raced in second place before taking it up with half a mile left to run and managed to maintain his advantage to the line.

The second race, a 0 to 55 handicap over seven furlongs, saw the 7/4 favourite Lord Of The East make very yard of the running and it was at that point that I started to pay extra attention. I decided I would watch the third race especially closely, just to confirm what was beginning to take shape.

The contest was a three-year-old claimer over six furlongs and I had already picked out a filly called Rancho Cucamonga as the most likely winner on my speed ratings, but the way the track was riding added further to my confidence, as she was not short of early pace and had a nice draw in stall four. I also decided to look harder and try and work out who was going to make the early running. I concluded that Norcroft, drawn in stall two, was the most likely one to set the pace, so apart from backing Rancho Cucamonga at 3/1, I also paired her with Norcroft in reverse exactas.

The result was never in doubt. Norcroft duly made the running with Rancho Cucamonga sitting on his tail, but eventually they swapped places before the pair pulled right away from the others to give the perfect result. I collected on the winner, whilst the exacta paid £18.80 for every £1 staked.

The fourth race on the card was a two-year-old maiden with little form to go on. I decided to sit it out, as these juveniles did not yet possess established running styles, being so inexperienced. For the record, the Evens favourite Sand Cat led within the first furlong and was never headed from that point, though he did only have a short head to spare at the line from a rival that had always been close to the pace.

The fifth race on the card was a three-year-old 0 to 70 handicap over five furlongs. Although not best drawn, the sweetly named Tartatartufata was the most likely early leader, so I backed her to a decent amount and watched her make every yard at odds of 4/1.

The last contest on the card was my least favourite type of race, a three-year-old maiden run over a mile with little form to go on, so I drew stumps as I could not be sure of who was likely to race up with the pace and I was well ahead anyway. As things turned out the race was won by a 13/2 newcomer called Bracklinn, who raced prominently throughout.

Situations like this are always worth looking out for and a bias exists at a large number of All-weather meetings, even if they are not always as pronounced as this one.

CHAPTER EIGHT

JOCKEYS AND TRAINERS

People's opinions with regard to jockeys and trainers are very subjective. For most who bet on horses regularly, the position of a jockey on their lists of favourites depends a fair amount on how many favours they have done you. How many of us have developed a soft spot for a jockey after we have won a decent sum on a horse they were aboard? We are drawn to their mounts for a period of time afterwards, sometimes for years, until we realise that we have given back the winnings several times over thanks to their losers.

A quick look at the statistics earlier in the book should be enough to persuade most people that following jockeys or trainers blind on the All-Weather is perilous, but it also shows that there is money to be made when you have the right people on your side.

Frankie Dettori's Magnificent Seven at the Ascot Festival of British Racing back in 1996 was a wonderful personal achievement, plus a great thing for racing in that it propelled the sport beyond its normal boundaries, but it also gave the whole idea of backing big-name jockeys blind some sort of perverted credence. How quick were the bookmakers to come on and offer odds about the same thing happening at the same meeting in the immediate years afterwards?

However, when it comes to All-Weather racing the best thing to do is discard a jockey or trainer's reputation for anything they may have achieved on turf. In fact without naming names, I will go as far as to say that one or two big-name jockeys have had some absolute nightmares when riding on the sand over the years. It's very difficult I know, but just as All-Weather racing is a different discipline for horses, it's also true with jockeys. A glance at the jockeys' statistics in Chapters Two, Three and Four does not show many household names near the top of each list, but those that are would be the ones I would rather have on my side on sand. They are the ones who have proved their worth on the surface, and that means everything.

As far as I am concerned, any jockey, no matter how high profile, starts with a clean slate once they start to ride on sand on a regular basis. Once they have become regulars on the All-Weather circuit, jockeys should be able to read the track at any given meeting and their strike-rate should benefit accordingly. Of course, there is no absolute guarantee that a rider will not make a mistake even if they have ridden at a track many times. In his book *Beyer On Speed* (Houghton Mifflin, New York 1993), Andy Beyer states that 'Bettors are totally at the mercy of jockeys' tactics, and the little pinheads are usually the last people at the racetrack to recognise a bias.' I wouldn't necessarily go quite that far, but I can see no excuse for a jockey getting beaten because they have persisted in racing on the part of the track which all the evidence points to as being disadvantaged.

So how do we go about using a jockey's record on sand to our advantage? The statistics shown earlier in this book together with those that appear on a regular basis in the racing press, such as the *Racing Post*, are obviously a big help, but the problem is that the jockey concerned will already have to have achieved something noteworthy in order to get a positive entry in the stats. The very best way to capitalise on the situation is to recognise it when it starts. What I mean is, if you follow All-Weather racing closely enough you tend to notice when a jockey starts to ride a few winners in a short space of time. Something 'clicks' in your head, at which point it is worth making a note of their name and then watching them more closely for a while. Occasionally you will find that their successes are a bit of a flash in the pan, or perhaps the winners they were aboard had so much in hand that anyone could have scored on them.

Fortunately, my own experience is that on enough occasions to make the expenditure of time worthwhile the reason why certain jockeys' names have made my notebook is because they have sorted out the idiosyncrasies of a certain track and have utilised that knowledge in order to increase their mounts' chances of winning. Here are two recent examples.

How many casual racegoers have heard of either George Baker or Chris Catlin? Not as many as have heard of Dettori or Fallon that's for sure, yet both Baker and Catlin have reached the top of the charts as far as I'm concerned because they have each learnt how to ride a track to their advantage.

For a few years Eddie Ahern was the master of the Lingfield Polytrack, but during the winter of 2004/5 George Baker moved up right alongside, winning several races thanks to some fine examples of judgement of pace and positioning of his horse. He became very adept at using the 'slingshot' into the home straight and it was two winning rides aboard a horse called Smokin Joe at the end of 2004 that catapulted him to the forefront of my mind. I was glad I took note, because he has done it many times since, often to my financial advantage. Notice that his level-stake profit at Lingfield between January 2002 and May 2005 is an impressive £63.75 to a £1 level stake, but perhaps even more relevant is that of the 29 winners he rode in that period, 18 were after November 2004. It's also worth noting that his record at Wolverhampton is pretty good too.

Chris Catlin has performed a similar feat at Wolverhampton in the short space of time since the new Polytrack surface was laid, as a level-stake profit of £67.33 will testify. The meeting that raised his profile with me took place on 13 December 2004 when he rode a double, and it was the second of those victories aboard an experienced sprinter call Sir Desmond in a ten-runner handicap over six furlongs that really caught my eye. Until then I hadn't come to any firm conclusions about the new surface, but after Catlin had held Sir Desmond up off a strong pace before delivering him right up the inside rail to win, I started to think a bit more about it. I quickly became convinced that it was no disadvantage to race against the inside rail, in fact at seemed to be an advantage, and that was totally at odds with the old Fibresand when doing so would have been fatal. It also told me that Chris Catlin had used his brain and was reading the track particularly well, a view that has been confirmed many times since.

One more thing worth noting about jockeys on the All-Weather is that over the years the winter season has been an effective nursery for nurturing riding talent. Several decent jockeys have come to prominence by riding a few winners on the sand and that number would probably be even greater if some trainers weren't so (understandably) keen for their apprentices to look after their claims and concentrate more on the turf season. That situation might change as the profile of sand racing improves, but in the meantime there will still continue to be at least one apprentice that really makes a name for him or herself during the winter before the wider racing world starts to take notice. In the winter of 2004/5 it was the turn of Adam Kirby to earn the title of 'apprentice find of the season' thanks to plenty of success, on Polytrack at least. On several occasions he showed some truly excellent judgement of pace, which will stand him in good stead in the years to come.

The advice here is that as soon as a 7lb claimer no-one has ever heard of starts to ride a winner or two on the All-Weather within a few days of each other, make a note of them because their 7lb claim will still put many ordinary punters off, whereas you will know different. Also make a note of any young rider who has been reported as having spent some time on a working holiday in America. The way they are taught to judge pace over there will be invaluable when they return here, especially when they ride on the sand.

As far as trainers are concerned, the statistics shown earlier in the book are again invaluable in trying to judge who's hot and who's not and, as with jockeys, a trainer's reputation is meaningless if they haven't proved that they can send out winners on the All-Weather on a regular basis. In fact, a big reputation can have beneficial consequences for the shrewd All-Weather punter. Just as the booking of a top jockey is likely to mean a horse starts shorter than it should be, a runner from a top stable is almost certain to be under-priced, especially if the animal involved has shown a bit of form on turf. This often means that the odds available on the genuine contenders are often greater than they should be and some wonderful value can be found.

There are some trainers who do especially well with horses they inherit from other yards, perhaps because they have the time to rekindle their enthusiasm or sort out a physical problem they may have. Tony Carroll, David Flood and Ron Harris are such examples, but there are many others and I always give their runners on sand a second look. That is not to say that a higher-profile trainer cannot enjoy excellent success on the sand. I wrote five years ago that Michael Jarvis's All-Weather runners were worth noting and as the trainer's statistics show, that is still the case.

I also mentioned Sir Mark Prescott as being almost completely dominant with horses that improve out of all recognition once they are stepped up to a trip more in line with their pedigrees. I suggested that horses such as Far Cry, Silent Warning and French Spice were good examples of this, but should also have pointed out that his masterly knack at placing his horses to maximum effect in general is unequalled, as Fall In Line's six victories in the space of 13 days at the beginning of 2004 will testify.

Probably the best example of how to capitalise on a trainer's skills remains the following example, which I used back in 2000. It portrays perfectly how a bit of forward thinking can be rewarded, both by a horse's connections and by those who know how to read a trainer's mind.

Some trainers have a team of All-Weather stalwarts in their yards that seem to appear year after year and they become very familiar names to anyone who follows racing on sand closely. Then there are horses who are purposely geared towards a winter campaign and only show their best form when the core All-Weather season comes around. Anything they do during the rest of the year is purely incidental, but despite the fact that the evidence is right there for anyone who has access to a horse's career history, the betting public can be impervious to its existence and the horse in question can go off at very tempting odds. One trainer who has enjoyed considerable success with this type of approach over the years is Patrick Haslam. The Middleham handler is one of the few I would describe as a 'thinking man's trainer' in that a shrewd approach towards the placement of horses has resulted in winners. Two horses in his care provide good examples of this.

The first was Pageboy, a son of Tina's Pet who raced until the age of 12 and who enjoyed a remarkable record in the middle of the 1990s. Although no world-beater, the horse had already been successful on turf and shown some ability on sand before he won the Too Many Cooks Handicap over six furlongs on the Lingfield Equitrack on 5 January 1995. He won off a mark of 62 then, but that soon rose to 69 whilst his turf mark reached a peak of 73 later on that year. Another 16 runs in 1995 yielded no further wins, but by the time 1996 came around the horse had fallen back to an All-Weather mark of 61.

For his first start of that year, Pageboy was sent to try and repeat his victory in the Too Many Cooks Handicap and this he did. However, unlike the previous year and despite a rise in the handicap, Pageboy managed to win twice more during that season, one on turf and one on sand at Wolverhampton off a mark of 67. The result of his Wolverhampton victory was that he started 1997 on a sand mark of 73, which would rule him out of a hat-trick bid in the Too Many Cooks Handicap as he was rated too highly. Instead he was sent for the higher-class Repulse Handicap over the same Lingfield six furlongs on 7 January 1997, and duly obliged. Not surprisingly his All-Weather mark took a battering and he shot up to 80. At the same time he seemed to lose his form on grass completely and he failed to make the frame in eight further starts that year. Consequently, his mark on both turf and sand gradually dropped and he started 1998 with an official rating on sand of 70, just enabling him to qualify for that year's Too Many Cooks Handicap on January 1st. He did it again, winning a race within the first week of the year over six furlongs on the Lingfield Equitrack for the fourth time in a row.

The sequence ended in 1999, but he was aged 10 by then and you can forgive an elderly gentleman most things!

Closer inspection of Pageboy's record also showed that he had a break of at least three months before each of those four victories, so there is little doubt that his success had been due to a bit of forethought and a bit of shrewd planning. The evidence was there for all to see for anyone who was able to see the horse's record over several years, so it follows that as people became wise to what was going on Pageboy's price should have been progressively shorter after each victory. Not a bit of it! His starting prices for those four victories were 7/4, 4/1, 4/1 and 8/1 respectively. It seems that most punters have very short memories and did not bother taking a wider view, and by concentrating on the horse's recent form all they saw was an exposed, out-of-form sprint handicapper returning from a break.

Remember that Pageboy had been unable to contest the 1997 Too Many Cooks Handicap due to his high rating? Well that year's renewal was won by 4/1 shot Ultra Beet, trained by a certain Patrick Haslam.

The other example of Mr Haslam's skill in placing his charges is with a horse called China Castle (see the Roll Of Honour on page 155). There are similarities with Pageboy, though his victories were rather more prolific and achieved at a higher level.

China Castle won as a two-year-old on sand at Southwell in August 1995, but had managed no better than sixth in six other races that year. Come the beginning of 1996, however, the son of Sayf El Arab started a remarkable sequence. He won his first three starts of that year, one on each of the three All-Weather tracks and all in January, the first off a mark of 54 and the last off 68. After a couple of defeats, he won again at Southwell the following month off 74, but did not manage another victory from ten further outings that year.

Come the beginning of 1997, China Castle's sand mark had dropped to a tasty 67 and he took full advantage by winning his first three starts of the year once again, all over middle distances at Southwell. After his third victory, his All-Weather mark shot up to 85 and he did not win again in 11 more starts that year, including one over hurdles. His run of defeats did result in his sand mark falling again though, and he started off 1998 rated 71.

He made his first appearance of the season back at Southwell and I remember it very well because I was there. He was strongly fancied, not least by me because I had just sussed the pattern to his form, but nothing went right for him in the race itself and he failed by a neck to get up and beat Alsahib. There were some long faces around the winner's enclosure afterwards, including mine, but Alsahib was a very decent sand performer at the time even though China Castle should probably have won. Still, he managed to win his next two starts, after which his sand mark went back up to 84 and he failed to win again from eight more starts that year.

It seemed to me that the world and his wife must have realised when the right time was to catch China Castle again, but I still awaited the start of 1999 with great anticipation. The time eventually arrived, and very soon I spotted China Castle amongst the entries for a valuable one mile three-furlong handicap at Southwell on 11 January, With the courage of my convictions, I decided to have a decent bet on the horse and, though I missed the early 6/1 about him, managed to get on at 5/1 which was still good value as he was eventually backed down to 3/1. Despite being almost brought down and knocked right back to the rear of the field starting down the back straight, China Castle came with a strong late run to get up near the line. I had lost several pounds in weight, but gained several pounds in cash and congratulated myself on spotting the horse's performance pattern.

China Castle went on to surprise even me after that though, as he continued his winning run for longer than in previous years, completing a four-timer in January and going on to win seven of his first nine starts that year, the last in March off a mark of 101. He even added a turf victory at Hamilton in July!

Things were a bit different after that though, he was absent from the track between July and November, which meant that on his return his All-Weather mark was a whopping 103. This meant that he was forced to race against the top sand performers such as Quintrell Downs and subsequent Winter Derby winner Zanay. Despite doing his best, he was not able to quite match horses of that calibre and it was not until he dropped to a mark of 85, some 16lb below his last All-Weather victory, that he returned to winning form at Lingfield on March 4th 2000 at the tempting odds of 11/2.

That is where the story ended in the first edition of this book, but as with all good yarns there was still more drama to come. Following a ten-month layoff, China Castle reappeared at the beginning of 2001 and went on to win another seven races from 11 outings on sand that year. The first five of those victories were in claimers, but the last one was in a valuable 0-95 handicap at Southwell, which showed that he still had what it takes. He only ran once more after that though, finishing fourth of 11 in a handicap at the same track in January 2002.

Not only do these examples show the value of trying to anticipate trainers' intentions, they also show the value of being able to view a greater proportion of a horse's form than just its last two or three outings, and looking deeper than just half a dozen recent form figures.

CHAPTER NINE

USING RATINGS

Using ratings is very much a question of personal taste. Some people like to use them to form the basis of a selection and others don't, whilst those that do use them do so in many different ways. If you are someone who uses ratings regularly, you will already understand much of what I'm about to say.

My own personal opinion is that ratings, whether they are performance ratings or speed ratings, are a very useful tool in sorting out the genuine contenders from the rest, but that they should not be adhered to blindly. Other factors, such as the draw, trainer intentions, early pace, suitability to the track, etc (all covered in other chapters) are of at least as great a significance as any rating, and it is only after these factors have been considered fully that ratings become significant. The type of ratings I'm talking about are those given to a horse for each individual performance, rather than a single overall 'master' rating, though this still has its place.

Some people prefer to calculate their own ratings and, in an ideal world, these are the most desirable to have as it means you have totally exclusive information, unless you decide to try and sell your ratings to someone else! If you want to try and produce your own performance or speed ratings, there are books on the market that will help you to do so and I can personally recommend it as a fascinating and rewarding venture, especially when your own hard labours identify a decent-priced winner! Most people don't have the necessary time to do this though, and instead rely on some form of published ratings, some of which still require a bit of adjustment before the final figure is arrived at.

There are several types of published ratings these days, such as in *Raceform, Timeform,* the *Racing Post* and so on, and these ratings are now available in both paper and electronic form (such as in computerised formbooks like *Raceform Interactive*). The ratings I know best are the performance and speed ratings published by the *Racing Post* and

Raceform (especially the Raceform Speed Figures as I have been compiling them since 2000). However, as I said before, whichever ratings people chose to use is a very personal choice.

If you are going to use ratings, how do you get the most out of them? The first thing to do is to decide whether you are going to use performance ratings or speed ratings as your preferred tool. Just to explain, a performance rating is one that defines the merit of the individual performance in terms of pounds in weight and has already been adjusted to the weight carried on the day. These ratings are shown under the heading of RPR, or Racing Post Rating, in *Raceform* publications and the *Racing Post*. When the horse runs again, the previous performance rating needs to be adjusted to take account of the weight to be carried in the forthcoming race. For example, if a Flat horse earns an adjusted performance rating of 74 and is due to carry 8st 7lb in his next start, the performance rating needs to be adjusted to a standard weight of say 10 stone. Our example horse is set to carry 21lb less than 10 stone in the upcoming race, so the adjusted rating for his previous performance is 95 (74 +21).

As I have said before, only previous runs on sand are of significance when analysing the form of an All-Weather race, so only the ratings allocated for races on sand should really be considered. The previous ratings of all horses due to take part in the race under review should be adjusted to the same standard weight. I've been using 10 stone in this chapter, though it doesn't matter what you use as long as it's the same for each runner. So for example, if a horse has earned adjusted past performance ratings of 63, 65, 74, 71 and 70 in his last five starts on sand, and he is due to carry 8st 13lb in his next outing, 15 needs to be added to each of those previous ratings (this being the difference between 10 stone and 8st 13lb) giving adjusted figures of 78, 80, 89, 86 and 85. Younger horses will require an amount to be deducted from these figures to account for immaturity, which means referring to the official weight-for-age scale shown at the end of this chapter.

However, that is only part of the story. Other useful information can be added to each rating, such as a pace symbol (most published results, especially in the trade press, will give a 'comment in running' which makes it easy to allocate a relevant symbol using the method outlined in Chapter Six). It's also worth adding the date of the race, the track, the race distance and the horse's finishing position, or indeed whatever information you feel is important. You then begin to see the conditions under which a horse puts up his or her best performances at a glance.

Here is a fictitious example. Imagine you are researching the form of a horse entered for an upcoming All-Weather race and he is due to carry 9st 3lb. You have looked up his last six sand starts and found that he has earned adjusted performance ratings of 67, 67, 64, 71, 72 and 69. After making the necessary weight adjustments, his form would look something like this.

Date	Track	Dist	Pos	Pace	Rating
22/01	Lingfield	6f	5	H	78
15/02	Lingfield	6f	4	H	78
28/02	Southwell	5f	7	H	75
14/03	Southwell	7f	1	L	82
01/04	Southwell	7f	1	L	83
17/04	Wolverhampton	6f	3	P	80

Notice that the ratings on the right have been increased by 11 from the original performance ratings, i.e. the difference between 10 stone and 9st 3lb.

If this horse was about to race over 7f at Southwell and his higher ratings were superior to the rest of the field, plus study of the pace symbols for each horse suggested he was very likely to get an early lead, then he would be a very interesting betting prospect. This may seem to be an extreme example, but in reality the majority of horses that run on sand have optimum conditions just like this, and this is where ratings are so valuable.

When you are able to see a horse's previous performances in this way, the conditions under which they are most favoured become very easy to spot, just like the horses shown in Chapter Five. Just how far back you are prepared to go in a horse's form in order to get an overall idea of its All-Weather profile is entirely up to you. The more runs you use, the more likely it is that you will be able to spot the circumstances of the horse's top performances. It all depends on how much time you are willing or able to spend.

Incidentally, computerised formbooks such as *Raceform Interactive* show past performances in a similar format to that shown above, but with a lot more information. They also do the necessary weight adjustments for you, thereby saving a great deal of time.

Speed ratings give a different view of a horse's performance. Whereas performance ratings are a purely subjective view of the ability of a horse, speed ratings use a constant called 'time'. As long as the time taken to run a race is measured accurately (now that we have electronic timing throughout Flat racing they have never been so accurate) then they can't be argued with. One minute thirty seconds is one minute thirty seconds no matter how much you fiddle with it and these race times can then be used to form the basis of speed ratings.

You will have already noticed how keen I am on using speed ratings as a major handicapping tool on sand. As I've said before, All-Weather racing is speed-orientated by its very nature, so it makes sense to use a method that can measure how fast a horse really is and can then be compared to other horses. You would be amazed how many supposed contenders become automatic rejects when you start to analyse their speed ratings, and these often include horses that are prominent in the betting. Some examples of this appear in Chapter Eleven.

Unlike with performance ratings, there is a choice to be made as to how you go about adjusting speed ratings for weight, if at all. The problem is that no-one can seem to agree on how much weight a horse carries affects its performance. It seems pretty obvious that carrying a substantial amount of extra weight compared to its last start should negatively affect its chance, but alas, life is not that simple. I have read many theories as to the effect of weight and have still to be convinced that you can apply a formula to adjust for weight that treats all horses as if they are the same.

When I first started compiling my own speed figures just under 15 years ago, I was desperate to find a formula of my own that I could use to adjust my speed figures for weight. I decided to do some testing to try and come up with the answer, so using my own All-Weather database I wrote a program that would work out how much a horse's speed rating was affected by every 1lb more or less weight that it carried compared to its previous start. I asked the program to analyse 1000 horses and left it to chug away. The results it produced with were a real eye--opener.

For every 1lb extra a horse had to carry, its speed rating was, on average, reduced by 0.4 of a point (on my scale one point equals one length). This works out to one length equalling 2.5lb. So far so good, but the problem was that for every 1lb less a horse had to carry, the speed figure was reduced again, this time by 0.3 of a point. Those horses that carried the same weight as in their previous starts actually saw an increase in their speed rating of 0.3 of a point. I tried the experiment again with a different set of horses and the results were similar. Whichever way you look at it, findings like these are very difficult to explain and I was not prepared to try and come up with some hotchpotch of a theory to try and fit the facts.

As a result of this research, I do not personally make any weight adjustments to my own speed ratings nor to the Split Second speed ratings I compile for *Raceform*, the reason being that I want to keep them as pure as possible. Factors such as the state of the track and class of race are taken into account, but I much prefer to make my own judgement on the likely effect of an increase or decrease in weight, just as I make my own judgement on the effect of the draw, early pace, fitness, trip, etc.

Another point worth mentioning is that while a big weight may well affect a steeplechaser racing over three and a half miles in bottomless ground, horses racing on sand never encounter those types of conditions and the extra weight has less of an opportunity to exacerbate the fatigue of an already tired horse. Also as we are only interested in All-Weather racing here, we can confidently place weight as a minor factor compared to those mentioned in the previous paragraph.

At least these days there is a choice as to whether you use weight-adjusted speed ratings or not. As I have said, the Split Second ratings in *Raceform* are not weight adjusted when published, though that is not to say some sort of personal weight adjustment cannot be applied to them afterwards, but the Topspeed ratings in *Racing Post* publications are already weight adjusted. So if you use the ones published in the *Weekender* for instance, then the procedure is exactly the same as for the performance ratings, except that no reference to the weight-for-age scale is necessary.

I do realise that doing what I've just suggested goes against the grain for most British punters. Adjusting ratings to take account of weight is so much part of us that it makes it rather difficult to just ignore it, but I believe it is the right strategy and perhaps the results of my own research will provide compelling evidence of that.

Another very British method of handicapping that does not sit too comfortably with using speed ratings is the use of collateral form. The idea is that if Horse A beats Horse B and Horse B goes on to beat Horse C, then if Horse A and Horse C were to meet, Horse A should come out best on a line through Horse B (assuming that the circumstances were identical for each contest). This line of thought appears in most form guides and it's strange that if the race didn't work out the way I've just suggested, the formbook 'may as well be thrown out of the window'. The problem is that the circumstances for each of the aforementioned contests are rarely the same and even if they were, horses do not stand still but progress and regress all the time.

Occasionally, when I have been discussing the likely outcome of an All-Weather race with another individual and the horse I like happens to have finished second in its previous start, the question I'm often asked is 'Who did it finish second to?' Often my reply is 'I don't know', which seems to totally stump the person I'm talking to. The reason I don't know is not because of some careless oversight on my part or pure laziness, it's because I don't really care who beat it. If my selection has higher speed figures than its rivals under conditions similar to those he will be racing under today, then that's good enough for me.

To give a comparison, I could finish second to an Olympic gold medallist in an eight-man race over 200 metres if the other six contestants were all over 70 years of age. A cursory glance at the form before my next start would reveal that I had finished second of eight to an Olympic Champion, which would make me a certainty against a field of average British club runners, but in reality because I'm totally unfit and sadly an ever-growing 18 stone in weight, I wouldn't have a prayer.

It sounds ludicrous doesn't it? But in reality the scenario I've just described is not so far from the way racing form is analysed in this country as you might think. The beauty of accurate speed ratings is that they summarise the performance of the individual horse without any reference to the company he has kept. If speed figures had been available for my fictional 200-metre race, they would have exposed me as far too slow to win any track event. Times are everything in athletics and anyone who follows that sport would soon know the truth about my real speed (or lack of it), as that is an integral part of athletics coverage. It's still less so in racing, though things are changing.

To illustrate the point, how often do you hear people say that it is dangerous to take conditions-race form at face value when analysing a handicap? The reason is simple. The conditions race was probably moderately run, meaning that modest horses were able to finish closer than they should and therefore making the form suspect. Anyone with access to speed ratings would know where they stood with such a race, whilst everyone else would be in the dark.

THE OFFICIAL SCALE OF WEIGHT, AGE & DISTANCE (FLAT)

The allowances are expressed as the number of pounds that is deemed the average horse in each group falls short of maturity at different dates and distances

Dist		Jan		Feb		Mar		Apr		May		Jun	
(fur)	Age	1-15	16-31	1 14	15-28	1-15	16-31	1-15	16-30	1-15	16-31	1-15	16-30
5	2	—	—	—	—	—	47	44	41	38	36	34	32
	3	15	15	14	14	13	12	11	10	9	8	7	6
6	2	—	—	—	—	—	—	—	—	44	41	38	36
	3	16	16	15	15	14	13	12	11	10	9	8	7
7	2	—	—	—	—	—	—	—	—	—	—	—	—
	3	18	18	17	17	16	15	14	13	12	11	10	9
8	2	—	—	—	—	—	—	—	—	—	—	—	—
	3	20	20	19	19	18	17	15	14	13	12	11	10
9	3	22	22	21	21	20	19	17	15	14	13	12	11
	4	1	1	—	—	—	—	—	—	—	—	—	—
10	3	23	23	22	22	21	20	19	17	15	14	13	12
	4	2	2	1	1	—	—	—	—	—	—	—	—
11	3	24	24	23	23	22	21	20	19	17	15	14	13
	4	3	3	2	2	1	1	—	—	—	—	—	—
12	3	25	25	24	24	23	22	21	20	19	17	15	14
	4	4	4	3	3	2	2	1	1	—	—	—	—
13	3	26	26	25	25	24	23	22	21	20	19	17	15
	4	5	5	4	4	3	3	2	1	—	—	—	—
14	3	27	27	26	26	25	24	23	22	21	20	19	17
	4	6	6	5	5	4	4	3	2	1	—	—	—
15	3	28	28	27	27	26	25	24	23	22	21	20	19
	4	6	6	5	5	4	4	3	3	2	1	—	—
16	3	29	29	28	28	27	26	25	24	23	22	21	20
	4	7	7	6	6	5	5	4	4	3	2	1	—
18	3	31	31	30	30	29	28	27	26	25	24	23	22
	4	8	8	7	7	6	6	5	5	4	3	2	1
20	3	33	33	32	32	31	30	29	28	27	26	25	24
	4	9	9	8	8	7	7	6	6	5	4	3	2

	Jul		Aug		Sep		Oct		Nov		Dec
1-15	16-31	1-15	16-31	1-15	16-30	1-15	16-31	1-15	16-30	1-15	16-31
30	28	26	24	22	20	19	18	17	17	16	16
5	4	3	2	1	1	—	—	—	—	—	—
33	31	28	26	24	22	21	20	19	18	17	17
6	5	4	3	2	2	1	1	—	—	—	—
38	35	32	30	27	25	23	22	21	20	19	19
8	7	6	5	4	3	2	2	1	1	—	—
—	—	37	34	31	28	26	24	23	22	21	20
9	8	7	6	5	4	3	3	2	2	1	1
10	9	8	7	6	5	4	4	3	3	2	2
—	—	—	—	—	—	—	—	—	—	—	—
11	10	9	8	7	6	5	5	4	4	3	3
—	—	—	—	—	—	—	—	—	—	—	—
12	11	10	9	8	7	6	6	5	5	4	4
—	—	—	—	—	—	—	—	—	—	—	—
13	12	11	10	9	8	7	7	6	6	5	5
—	—	—	—	—	—	—	—	—	—	—	—
14	13	12	11	10	9	8	8	7	7	6	6
—	—	—	—	—	—	—	—	—	—	—	—
15	14	13	12	11	10	9	9	8	8	7	7
—	—	—	—	—	—	—	—	—	—	—	—
17	15	14	13	12	11	10	9	6	8	7	7
—	—	—	—	—	—	—	—	—	—	—	—
19	17	15	14	13	12	11	10	9	9	8	8
—	—	—	—	—	—	—	—	—	—	—	—
21	20	16	16	14	13	12	11	10	10	9	9
—	—	—	—	—	—	—	—	—	—	—	—
23	22	20	18	16	14	13	12	11	11	10	10
1	—	—	—	—	—	—	—	—	—	—	—

CHAPTER TEN

BETTING OPPORTUNITIES

Whenever most people place a bet on a horse, they do so because they hope to win. On the other hand, some people place a bet on a horse because they expect to win. The whole reasoning behind this book is that, after reading it, anyone who places a bet on an All-Weather race will belong to the second group rather than the first. This is because that by merely taking in any or all of the information or hints that have appeared herein, you will know more than, and consequently have the advantage over, 95% of the people who will also be placing an investment in such a race.

I ought to mention at this point that the dramatic expansion of the betting exchanges in the past five years has changed the betting world for ever and provided another major weapon in the hands of the thinking and well-informed punter. Despite some disturbing and controversial stories having made the pages of the racing press in the last few years, the development of the exchanges has to be seen as a good thing from the All-Weather punter's point of view. The whole point of this book is that we delve that bit deeper and use methods that the everyday punter is unable or unwilling to use, such as sifting out the sand form from the turf, using draw statistics together with the pace angle, etc.

Naturally the other major aspect of the exchanges is that you can lay horses to lose and all the way through this book I have been banging on about opposing vulnerable, short-priced favourites. The type of horse I particularly like to home in on are those with good form on turf making their sand debuts, or horses that have tried sand a few times in the past and shown nothing, yet are a short price now because they are returning to sand after showing smart form on turf. Occasionally I will also lay horses whom my statistics show are starting from a bad draw, provided their price is short enough, and will do the same where my pace statistics show that the individual's style of running is likely to be a disadvantage. I especially wish the exchanges had been around when Centre Stalls ran in the 1997 Wulfrun Stakes!

Of course there are people on the exchanges who are particularly well-informed one way or another. It would be naïve to believe otherwise, but fortunately there is still plenty of (and I hate to use the phrase) 'mug money' being thrown about which means that some cracking bets can be found. This situation is not confined to the exchanges though. Lazy punters abound throughout the betting world and money can be made if you take the time and effort whilst others blindly follow what they read in the papers. I have capitalised on this situation many times, both via the betting exchanges and traditional bookmakers, such as when my draw statistics show there to be a significant bias. For instance, as the draw statistics in Chapter Four show, low draws over sprint trips at Wolverhampton enjoy a significant advantage, but how much of an advantage does not seem to be yet reflected in the prices of the horses starting from those stalls.

Here is an example of what I mean. On 25 April 2005 there was a 12-runner three-year-old handicap run over six furlongs at Wolverhampton. The 15/8 favourite was a horse called Depressed who was due to start from stall five, which was fair enough. However, in stall one was a filly called Lady Vee, trained by former top jump jockey Peter Niven and ridden by 3lb claimer Tom Eaves. Her form figures from four outings on turf were 8500, so it was no surprise that she was an unconsidered 33/1 shot. Granted her form was poor, but so pronounced was the advantage enjoyed by low draws according to my statistics that I was very tempted to back her. A little more research told me that she had at least shown a bit of early speed in a couple of her starts, which I felt was important as once again my statistics told me that horses who were able to race prominently were especially suited by these conditions. I decided to have a bit on her, both on the exchanges and with a couple of traditional bookmakers.

Once the race was under way, everything went perfectly. Lady Vee was able to take a handy position from her inside stall and maintained her effort to get up near the line and win by half a length. Again a little bit of time and effort and using all the information at my disposal had landed me a four-figure sum. Incidentally, as if to demonstrate the bias towards those drawn on the inside, the first six home came from the six lowest stalls.

As I said earlier, many punters look for shortcuts in order to find a selection, such as by blindly following their pet racing tipster or by backing the horse with the highest 'master' rating, with no research into where and under what circumstances that rating was achieved. This is not meant as criticism by any means. People often lead busy lives and don't have the time to delve deeply enough into every horse's record. It is all very well for some faceless expert to start declaring that you shouldn't do this or do that, but real life does not work that way.

Having said all of that, I can only state what I believe to be the consequences of trying to take shortcuts to making a final selection. Form books, either paper or computerised, performance ratings, speed ratings and statistics are all useful tools in arriving at the eventual goal, that of backing a winner. If you are not able to dedicate a reasonable amount of time analysing the race you want to bet on, you will have about as much chance of backing the winner as the vast majority of people betting in the same race, and that usually means that in the long run, your money is on a one-way ticket towards the bookmakers.

The beauty of All-Weather racing is that you can more or less treat it as a separate sport and don't have to worry too much about the thousands of races that are run on turf when it comes to analysing the form. So what constitutes a decent betting prospect when it comes to a race on sand?

As I've demonstrated in earlier chapters, one area that can be exploited is in All-Weather maiden races for older horses, but only when there is plenty of previous form on show. These races often contain a horse with placed form on turf and who may well come from a big yard. Leaving aside those trainers with a knack for producing All-Weather maiden winners at the first time of asking, such a move can often be in desperation. The animal concerned is quite unlikely to be improving and as a last resort the horse has been switched onto the sand in order to try and break its duck. If the field also contains at least one horse that has shown some sort of ability on the same sand surface as they are about to race on, then a real opportunity exists. You just need some further research before isolating a selection, such as ratings, draw positions, etc. The market will probably have the classy turf horse in at a short price, and if so you can afford to back more than one of the dangers, or lay the favourite on the exchanges.

A similar scenario occurs in handicaps when a horse with winning form on turf makes its All-Weather debut. The horse is almost certainly going to be too short in the betting as no-one really knows how it will cope with racing on sand for the first time, especially if it's taking on rivals with solid sand form.

I have occasionally backed a horse making its sand debut as long as it has shown some form on turf, but only when those that have raced on sand before have shown form well below the standard required to win at today's level. Speed figures are once again an invaluable tool in identifying such horses, and this type of positive-negative thinking can be of real value. In the same way that speed ratings can isolate the genuine contenders in a race, they can also tell you that the value of previous form on sand is so low that these horses are going to be susceptible to a sand newcomer with any ability at all.

There are potentially even more lucrative ways of guaranteeing a decent return when your judgement proves to be correct. If your pre-race analysis tells you that there are two or three genuine contenders with a decent chance on their previous sand form, but the favourite is a sand newcomer, then the shrewd move is to combine your shortlist horses in computer straight forecasts or Tote exactas. Then when as so often happens, the turf hotpot is completely unable to show its best form on this new surface and your selections fill the first two places, the rewards emanating from your correct opinion will be multiplied several times over.

Whilst I don't personally bet with the Tote very often these days, there is a bet that I believe provides a wonderful chance to make money by making the most out of the type of situation just described. That bet is the Tote Placepot. The reason why I believe the Placepot is such a great weapon in the armoury of the shrewd All-Weather punter is that most people who have a go at it are not shrewd All-Weather punters. Again that horrible phrase 'mug money' can be used when a large part of the Placepot pool is made up by people who are only doing the bet for a bit of fun. In other words they are hoping for a sizeable return for a relatively small stake. The National Lottery works in much the same way.

As a consequence, a lot of the people who invest in this bet have arrived at their selections by blindly following the tipsters in the national newspapers or their racecards, in fact using any method except the more detailed type of study outlined in this book. The result is that these punters will get it wrong if the tipster gets it wrong, and even if they get it right, the dividend will almost certainly be low because heavily tipped horses will have made the frame throughout the meeting. By taking an alternative view, however, if you get it right you will often find that not many will have survived along with you, and a tasty dividend is the likely outcome.

I am not suggesting that you take an alternative view just for the sake of it. If your research tells you that the forecast favourites are going to have a good day, then there is no point in doing the Placepot at all, especially if you perm several lines, as you may still make a loss on the bet even if one of your lines hits the target. The best opportunity with the Placepot is when there is at least one vulnerable favourite lurking in the card, the sort of horse that is likely to have many people banking on it in the Placepot.

Five years ago I described a Lingfield meeting from 1997 to demonstrate just such a scenario, but just to show that these methods are as effective now as they have ever been, here is a more recent example.

I wasn't able to attend the Lingfield meeting on 17 May 2005 in person, but always look carefully at any All-Weather card to see if I can find a bet. Having scoured the card fully, I felt I had found a couple of favourites to take on. I should mention at this point that this was a Regional meeting, not my favourite type of racing, but one thing you do normally get at these fixtures is decent size fields and as a result the market tends to be wide open. As with any type of race though, a vulnerable favourite in a banded race is still going to attract a lot of support in the Placepot and in my opinion here we had at least two. The horses involved weren't really short enough to lay on the exchanges, so I decided to do a Placepot perm and take these two shaky favourites on that way.

It was therefore ironic that in the very first race was our old friend Baytown Flyer. Remember the race I described back in Chapter Six where she was such a cracking bet under the conditions that prevailed at Wolverhampton on that day? Well here she was running again just 24 hours later, but this time she was starting from stall ten in a 13-runner field over a course and distance where such a draw was a major disadvantage. Add to that the fact that she was up against at least two other front-runners then she had to be bad value at 11/4. I did include her in my Placepot perm just in case she happened to find herself with an uncontested early lead, but I also put in two other horses that were major contenders on my ratings and were also drawn better, namely Coronado Forest and Wodhill Be.

When the stalls eventually opened, Baytown Flyer stood still and lost a good six lengths, thereby ending any chance she may have had. There was no way I could have predicted that, and was certainly not complaining once Coronado Forest and Wodhill Be finished first and third respectively. The shortest price of three to make the frame was 15/2, so it was certainly the sort of start I wanted.

The second race was more straightforward. I included the favourite Sewmore Character as he appeared to have a class advantage over his rivals, but he was also starting to show signs of decline, so I also added Savernake Brave because he had solid form at this level on this track. Predictably Sewmore Character managed to get himself trapped amongst horses, but he didn't convince me that he was trying all that hard when he did get out into the clear. Fortunately, Savernake Brave crept into third place and as he was the shortest price of the three to make the frame at 9/1, we were now really rolling!

The third race on the card contained the other vulnerable favourite. Ulshaw had always been the sort of horse that needed a decent test of stamina in my opinion. In fact in his younger days he had been something of a standing dish over two miles on Fibresand at Wolverhampton and the only reason he was such a short price for this was that he had recently been in good form on turf. One thing he certainly didn't have was any worthwhile form at Lingfield. Surely one mile and five furlongs around here wasn't going to suit him, so he had to be rejected. I took him on with three horses in this particular leg, though ironically I ended up with him included in my bet when one of my three selections, Free Style, was withdrawn, thereby being forced on to the favourite. I was still relying more on my two other selections though, namely Frontlinefinancier and One Upmanship, both of whom seemed more likely to be suited by these conditions.

As things turned out, One Upmanship merely flattered to deceive, but Frontlinefinancier did manage to finish second with the favourite Ulshaw a never-nearer eighth. Three races down and no favourites placed!

The favourite was placed in the fourth race, which is just as well as she was one of my two selections for the contest, whilst the other one Flapdoodle only beat one home. I was particularly pleased to get through this leg, as it looked a horrible little banded sprint, one of those races you look through and deduce that nothing can possibly win!

The fifth race wasn't much easier and as a result I had included three in the Placepot. Lillianna and Tintawn Gold could only manage fourth and sixth respectively, but fortunately my other selection Lady Taverner crept into third place behind the favourite Halcyon Magic, so I was still alive.

And so to the last leg. I had come to the conclusion that those at the head of the market all had solid chances, particularly the favourite Blessed Place who just had to be included despite his modest winning record. As you can see from his profile shown below, his speed figures were far superior to his rivals, he was drawn nicely in stall one, and just look at his sand form coming into the race and assess his chances in view of the draw and front-runner statistics shown further down. Incidentally, my other Placepot selection Tosco was drawn in stall number four.

5-00 RETAIL TRUST WELFARE SERVICES APPRENTICE BANDED STAKES (0-45) (7) 3YO+
6 furlongs   Par = 97   12 runners

3 1 BLESSED PLACE			9-0(T)		D J S FFRENCH DAVIS			R KEOGH(5)		
11 JAN 03	LING	5	SD	6H	3	10	8-11	7	P	89
20 JAN 03	WOLV	6	SW	6H	2	12	8-12	6	P	84
05 FEB 03	LING	6	SD	4M	5	12	9-0	8	P	94
25 FEB 03	LING	5	SW	5H	3	10	8-8	4	P	94
04 MAR 03	LING	5	SD	4M	2	9	8-12	1	L	97
05 MAR 03	LING	5	SW	4H	1	6	8-8	2	L	100
17 JAN 04	LING	5	SD	6H	8	9	11-0	2	P	77
16 FEB 04	WOLV	5	VS	6H	11	11	9-7	6	P	71
26 FEB 04	LING	6	SD	6H	13	13	9-6	12	L	90
04 JUN 04	WOLV	5	SD	6H	8	13	9-8	6	L	84
08 NOV 04	SOUT	5	SD	7B	9	14	9-1	11	P	87
24 JAN 05	WOLV	6	SD	7B	5	12	9-0	12	H	96
28 FEB 05	LING	6	SD	7B	7	11	9-0	10	H	94
31 MAR 05	LING	5	FT	7B	3	10	8-12	3	P	92
18 APR 05	WOLV	6	FT	7B	2	12	9-0	7	L	93
28 APR 05	LING	6	VF	7B	2	11	9-7	9	L	96

12-month draw record for 6 furlongs

Draw No	Runners	Winners	%
1	82	10	12
2	83	4	5
3	80	2	3
4	83	13	16
5	81	6	7
6	81	13	16
7	80	7	9
8	85	10	12
9	77	7	9
10	69	6	9
11	62	3	5
12	53	5	9

Front Runners Impact Value = 1.8
Prominent Horses Impact Value = 1.1
Hold Up Horses Impact Value = 0.8

As you can see, Blessed Place had a good draw judging by the statistics and his style of running was going to be suited to the track. The only other horse with pretensions to being a front-runner was drawn in the very outside stall, so Blessed Place was beginning to look a good thing and I managed to get on at 3/1 just before the off, even though I hadn't originally intended to do any other bets apart from the Placepot. Fortunately Blessed Place burst from the stalls in front and never looked like getting caught. My other selection Tosco finished third.

My Placepot comprised of 216 lines at a unit stake of 25p, costing £54 in all. I had been successful with four lines (having managed to get two into the frame in legs one and six), which meant that I had £1 worth of winning tickets in my possession. The dividend was £1,301.70 to a £1 stake, not bad for a moderate Regional meeting and due in no small part to spotting a couple of vulnerable favourites beforehand.

CHAPTER ELEVEN

DIARY 2005

Saturday 12 March – Wolverhampton

When I started writing the diary that appeared in the original book five years ago, I went into it at the very top of my game punting-wise, and therefore brimming full of confidence. This time around however, things had proved very tough in the early months of 2005, with winners difficult to find and races becoming more and more tactical, especially at the two Polytrack venues. That wasn't the whole story though. One of the main problems with my betting had been the re-emergence of the silly errors which I thought I had eradicated, such as blindly going for the top horse on my ratings too often rather than using the figures as the useful starting point they are meant to be.

Still, at least I felt I had spotted the gremlins in time and I was aware that this diary was going to be included in this updated version of the book no matter how things eventually worked out, so the pressure was most definitely on. I should mention at this point that whilst forcing yourself to go through your betting records may be tedious, it doesn't half force you to face up to your punting demons and I would strongly urge anyone who bets seriously, as many writers on this subject have done before me, to keep records of every single bet you make. If you do that, then the silliest mistakes are very likely to magically disappear, otherwise they tend to come back and haunt you.

You may also notice that during the period of the new diary, unlike in the first version, I kept my stakes to a uniform £40, which has been my average stake for the past few years. There are two reasons for this. Firstly, I didn't want a situation to arise where an increased stake on one or two decent-priced winners distorted the overall running total, as desirable as that may be for my bank. Also, theoretic level stakes are often used to test the prowess or otherwise of tipsters, such as in the *Racing Post* naps competitions, though of course in this case there was nothing theoretical about the hard cash I was going to be playing with. In other words I wanted this diary to be a test of my methods, not my staking plan.

So what follows are my exploits at the track for a series of All-Weather fixtures during the spring and summer of 2005, beginning with Wolverhampton's main fixture of the year featuring the £50,000 Littlewoods Bet Direct Lincoln Trial.

I don't normally bet on every race on the card and probably shouldn't have done here, but this looked a tasty meeting and I had an opinion of some sort on all eight races.

My take on the first contest, a three-year-old sprint claimer, was that it was very definitely a two-horse race.

2-05	BET DIRECT NO Q ON 08000 93 66 93 CLAIMING STAKES (F4) 3YO							
5.1 furlongs		Par = 96			8 runners			
AW FORM	NAME	BEST	LAST SIX					
002-1212	HIAMOVI	96W05	76S08	88S05	96W05	89W05	91W06	92L05
7413-730	AZUREE	96L06	87W06	91W06	96L06	79S06	86L06	90L07
17-56	NOVA TOR	95L06			83S05	88S05	91L06	95L06
11-6	LITTLE BISCUIT	90S05				83W05	90S05	77L05
648-	DUCAL DIVA	85W05				82S05	85W05	78W05
46	RUBY MUJA	84L05					84L05	69L05
470-0	ELLIS CAVE	83S07			83S07	77S06	65S06	80W06

There was nothing clever about that as the betting also suggested it was a two-horse race, the pair hovering at around the 6/4 mark, but unfortunately they weren't big enough prices to make it worthwhile backing them both. I was happy to eliminate Azuree as she hadn't been at her best so far in 2005 and saw it as a straight match between Hiamovi and Nova Tor. I liked the way Nova Tor's speed figures were gradually moving upwards and further improvement would take her above the par for the class, but Hiamovi had form on the track, which Nova Tor hadn't. The clincher for me though was the draw. Hiamovi was drawn in stall one, whilst Nova Tor had the outside stall seven and my stats told me that an inside draw was preferable, so I took £70-£40 about Hiamovi.

Despite starting from the inside stall, Hiamovi ended up making his effort wide of Nova Tor, but could never quite get past the filly who maintained a half-length advantage to the line. Not the best of starts, but I was sort of right in that the pair had the race completely to themselves.

The second race was much more competitive, a £20,000 handicap over six furlongs.

2-35	BET DIRECT ON 0800 32 93 93 HANDICAP (0-100) (C1) 4YO+							
6 furlongs		Par = 107					11 runners	
AW FORM	NAME					BEST LAST SIX		
1614-212	RUSSIAN SYMPHONY	109L06	98W07	104W07	100W07	100W07	109L06	103W06
61-43213	ROMAN MAZE	108L06	97W06	95W07	102L07	108L06	106W06	101W06
2/03-2	RYDAL	108L06			95L07	95L07	108L06	105W06
/32184-1	KINGSMAITE	107W06	100S07	103W06	103W07	100W06	98S05	107W06
/22-1232	HIDDEN DRAGON	107W05	104L07	101L07	107S05	106S06	101L05	107W05
3123-121	KATIYPOUR	107L10	106L08	104L08	105L10	96L07	105L07	106L06
2103-R31	QUIET TIMES	107L06	107S05	92W06	102S05	0S05	104W06	107L06
70-03927	HURRICANE COAST	107L06	99L07	97L07	105L06	98L07	105W06	99W06
094-5603	TIME N TIME AGAIN	105W05	95S05	95W06	100S06	98S05	98W06	101W06
	DOITNOW							

This looked a very tight affair on the speed figures as races like this tend to be, but my eye had been drawn to Katiypour. Whilst most of the horses in this particular race had always been sprinters, Katiypour had been running over middle distances in recent years, but had shown improved form since being dropped down in trip in his recent starts. Indeed he had won a decent handicap over six furlongs at Lingfield in his most recent outing, the first time he had ever raced over so short a trip in his whole career. He was therefore a relatively unexposed sprinter compared to his rivals and he was also nicely drawn in stall four, so I was happy to take £160-£40.

I had been able to eliminate several of his main dangers on account of the draw, but I was afraid of Quiet Times in stall one who had been racing in Dubai since winning a decent conditions event at Lingfield in his last domestic outing, so I also took £280-£40 about him.

I soon knew the fate of my Quiet Times bet. He had refused to come out of the stalls at Southwell earlier in the year and although he did eventually get going this time, he gave his rivals a four-length start and you can't afford to do that at this level and hope to get away with it. Katiypour also had plenty to do starting up the home straight and only had Quiet Times behind him, but he then found a very smart turn of foot to cut down all of his rivals and win by half a length from Rydal, who did very well to finish so close from an outside draw.

We were now off and running, so I was very much looking forward to the rest of the afternoon, starting with a £10,000 handicap over the extended two miles.

AW FORM	NAME	BEST	LAST SIX					
3-10	**BET DIRECT ON THE FA CUP HANDICAP (0-85) (D2) 4YO+**							
16.5 furlongs			Par = 105	13 runners				
114-01	GARDEN SOCIETY	109W13		105W12	109W13	75W13	91L12	88L16
9-219193	BROUGHTON KNOWS	108S12	99W13	92L16	91W12	102W12	96L12	100S14
11-34228	BIENHEUREUX	107W12	102W12	99L13	101W12	91L13	107W12	97L12
07114-76	VICTORY QUEST	107S14	0S12	100S14	103S16	88W16	81S11	98S12
52-43167	EASTBOROUGH	106W12	84L12	100L10	94L12	97W12	106W12	103L10
45/8-45	CONSIDINE	106W12		81W06	77S06	80S08	106W12	82L16
21-1	SERBELLONI	105W13				102W09	84L12	105W13
45321-24	MACARONI GOLD	104L16	87W16	100S16	88W16	102S14	102S16	88L16
/428-127	BIG BERTHA	104L16	80L13	100W12	93L12	103W12	104L16	87L16
11831-99	SUN HILL	104L12	99W16	92W16	87W16	75W13	104L12	98W09
3/0-	MANA D'ARGENT	103S14					103S14	82W13
53/4-16	TURN 'N BURN	102L12		89L08	93L08	102L12	91L12	101L12
0	OBAY	91L12						91L12

This contest is one of the best staying races of the year on sand, which demonstrates the quality, or lack of it, of this category on the artificial surfaces. Not that many horses truly see out the longer trips on sand, especially on the slower surfaces, so previous winners over the distance are usually what I look for first. Garden Society had won over the trip at Lingfield in his previous start, albeit in a very slowly run race, but had shown earlier in the winter that he was much better suited by a strongly run race. With the size and quality of this field, I was convinced that something would set out and make it a true pace, so I took £160-£40 about Garden Society and went to stand next to the stalls in order to watch the start.

How wrong I was about the likely pace. As soon as the race was under way, it was obvious that this was going to be yet another All-Weather staying event blighted by a slow pace. That proved to be a big help to Serbelloni, who was stepping up in trip, though admittedly he was an improving sort. Garden Society ran him very close though, getting within a head of the favourite despite the race not being run to suit.

The next race on the card was the highlight of the afternoon, the Lincoln Trial over the extended one-mile trip.

AW FORM	NAME	BEST	LAST SIX						
			3-45 LITTLEWOODS BET DIRECT LINCOLN TRIAL HERITAGE HANDICAP (0-105) (B1) 4YO+						
			8.6 furlongs — Par = 109 — 13 runners						
/111110-	VORTEX	114W08	105W08	98L08		104W08	101W08	114W08	97L104
215/3/3	IONIAN SPRING	111L10		111L10	106W12	105S12	107S12	105W1	106L10
15410-74	LYGETON LAD	110L07		104L07	105L07	104L08	99L07	100W08	106L10
1111-2	CONSONANT	109W08			108W08	89W08	109W08	105L10	107L10
3/6-11	SRI DIAMOND	108L10				105L07	86L08	95L08	108L10
11	NIGHT AIR	108L08						101W07	108L08
9-40	DANDOUN	107W08					99L08	107W08	83S07
1-	APPALACHIAN TRAIL	106W08							106W08
15	PRINCE TUM TUM	106W06						106W06	103L06
/6112-87	RED LANCER	106S12		97W08	98S11	105W09	106S12	88L10	102L12
1-0	ALWAYS ESTEEMED	104L08						104L08	62L10
6/11/	KING'S THOUGHT	103L08					93L10	103L08	102L08
	WING COMMANDER								

This looked like being a cracking contest and the one I liked was Night Air, whose speed figure for his recent Lingfield win was close to the par for the grade. He was also unexposed on sand and still improving, so there was a very real chance he could go even higher, whereas those near the top of the listing had rather levelled off. Many people seemed to agree with me though, probably his form figures and the booking of Jamie Spencer had made him look attractive anyway, and he was put in as favourite at around 3/1 when I had been hoping for at least double that.

Some people were worried about him being drawn in stall 12 in a 13-runner field, but my draw stats showed that plenty of winners had come from that draw over the trip, so it shouldn't really be a problem. In these circumstances the horrible word 'value' tends to come to the fore and there are some who would have changed their minds and backed something else when they found out his price. My view was that Night Air still looked the likeliest winner so I hid my disappointment and took £120-£40.

I had gone down to watch the start of the race once again and as soon as the contest got under way it was obvious Jamie Spencer was going to have to bring Night Air from well off the pace. Rounding the home turn he was starting to make progress, but still seemed to have an awful lot to do and even by the time the field passed me with about half a furlong left to run, Vortex appeared to hold an unassailable lead, but Night Air was really finishing strongly down the outside of the track and managed to get up to win by a neck.

Although I had collected, I didn't feel I had capitalised as much as I would have liked due to the skinny price, which is an emotion we all experience on a regular basis as punters, but I was pleased that my view of Night Air as a progressive individual had been proved correct.

The next race on the card was a three-year-old maiden and the choice seemed perfectly straightforward.

4-20 BET DIRECT 1/4 FIRST FIVE AT CHELTENHAM MAIDEN STAKES (D3) 3YO								
8.6 furlongs			Par = 100	13 runners				
AW FORM	NAME	BEST	LAST SIX					
5-342	DON PASQUALE	104W08			93L07	96W09	96W09	104W08
2-2	INDEBTED	96L08					96L08	87L10
78	HIGH	89L08					89L08	86W07
0	DINNER DATE	86W09						86W09
9-0	INDIAN SKY	86L07					83L07	86L07
7	RONSARD	84W08						84W08
8-6	PENNAUTIER	82W06					82W06	53S08
7-	MOONSTRUCK	80L08						80L08
0	KING MARRAKECH	75L07						75L07
	ZAGORA							
	MYSTERIOSA							
	FAMILY 'N FRIENDS							
	LANKAWI							

Usually I'm not a great fan of All-Weather maidens for older horses when there is limited form to go on, but this contest appeared to be an exception as it seemed to be a straight match between two horses, one of which I didn't like the look of. In situations like this, you can get tremendous value on your selection if you believe there is a flaw in the credentials of the only conceivable danger. The one I didn't like on this occasion was Indebted who had pulled her chance away in a Lingfield maiden in her previous start and the form looked weak in any case, as can be seen by the moderate speed figure.

I did like Don Pasquale though, despite him apparently looking more exposed than his market rival. His form had a progressive look to it and he already had course form, so I considered a bet of £100-£40 tremendous value on what was basically a toss of a coin.

Again I went down to view the start of the race, which is well worth doing if you get the chance as you really feel the excitement of the contest as it gets under way. Having said that, although you may be close to the early action you can't always see what is happening side-on and on this occasion being able to do so would have proved enlightening. I remember thinking as the field reached halfway that Jamie Spencer was giving Don Pasquale an awful lot to do and he never looked like making up the ground, eventually being beaten six lengths into third place behind Indebted. It later transpired that Don Pasquale had suffered interference just after the start, which I hadn't been able to see, and that was the reason why he found himself right at the back of the field.

Even though things hadn't gone to plan this time, this type of situation is still worth keeping an eye open for. This was a two-horse race as far as I was concerned and 5/2 was still great value despite the result.

I was bruised if not beaten and the next contest had looked a no-bet race to me right up until close to the off.

4-50	LITTLEWOODS BET DIRECT CONDITIONS STAKES (C1) 4YO+								
7.1 furlongs			Par = 107	8 runners					
AW FORM	NAME	BEST	LAST SIX						
200-3170	TE QUIERO	114W08	101L07	98L07	113S08	110S07	91W08	91S07
1791-125	MOAYED	110W08	99S05	104L06	109L07	110W08	106L06	101W08
82-21111	SET ALIGHT	106S07	98W07	101S07	99S07	100S07	103S07	106S07
121436-	SAMUEL CHARLES	104W07	103L08	100W08	104W07	92W07	99W07	95W07
621-4044	MISTRAL SKY	104L06	100W06	100W07	100W07	96L07	103W06	101W06
32271141	ZORN	100S06	93S06	89W07	96S06	100S06	93S06	95S06
6-	RAHEED	94L08						94L08

Moayed had been one of the top performers on sand during the winter and I expected him to be odds-on even before his probable main danger Chateau Nicol was withdrawn. I was convinced Moayed would be totally unbackable, so imagine my surprise when I saw some of the on-course bookmakers offering 5/4 about him, mainly due to continued market support for Te Quiero, a horse that had never finished closer than seventh in eight previous tries on Polytrack. This was too good a chance to miss, so I took £50-£40 about Moayed.

Unfortunately this was another race where anything that could go wrong did go wrong. Moayed was held up off the pace as usual, but got hampered when trying to get a run up the inside of weakening rivals on the home bend and then took a broadside from Te Quiero when trying to make progress around the outside straightening up for home. He stayed on strongly down the straight, but Mistral Sky had got first run on him and held on to win by a diminishing head.

I probably shouldn't have played in the next race, but I was feeling sore after Don Pasquale and Moayed, so I took the plunge.

5-20	BET DIRECT ON CHANNEL 4 PAGE 613 HANDICAP (DIV I) (0-85) (D2) 4YO+							
7.1 furlongs			**Par = 105**	**10 runners**				
AW FORM	NAME	BEST			LAST SIX			
31-1123	WESSEX	112S08	98W06	100S07	107S08	105W07	112S08	111S08
/761/19-	UHOOMAGOO	112S07	98S08	82S07	88S08	101W07	112S08	102L07
586-2485	SOBA JONES	110S06	94W06	97S05	103S06	99W06	91S06	98S06
22254-34	TEMPLET	108W08	103W08	103W09	99W08	104S08	108W08	105W08
39-415	NORTHERN DESERT	104L07		104L07	94W08	103L07	101L08	102L08
52-65804	SILENT STORM	103W08	100W07	103W08	102L06	98L07	57S06	99L08
08-45813	XPRES DIGITAL	103S06	86W06	99S06	96W06	94W07	103S06	100S06
9-666	FOLIO	103L07			87L08	99L08	102L08	103L07
0-0	DESERT OPAL	82W08					58W07	82W08
	ODDSMAKER							

I knew that Wessex had the worst of the draw, but he was also in great form and there were no doubts about his ability to handle the track. The only danger I could see was Uhoomagoo, who had shown nothing in a couple of recent outings in Dubai and always needed a strongly run race in order to show his best. Looking at each horse's running styles, I couldn't see him getting that in this event, so I took £110-£40 about Wessex.

This was a very strange race as Wessex flew out of the stalls from his outside draw and went off like a bat out of hell. By halfway he had established a big advantage and I'm sure that several people around me believed the contest was over, but as I said earlier, Uhoomagoo was going to require a breakneck pace if he was going to score and Wessex had set the race up perfectly. Inevitably Uhoomagoo cut Wessex down inside the last furlong and bolted right away to win by three-and-a-half lengths.

I was very confused by what had just happened, but hopefully the final race of the day would prove more straightforward.

5-50	BET DIRECT ON CHANNEL 4 PAGE 613 HANDICAP (DIV II) (0-85) (D2) 4YO+							
7.1 furlongs			**Par = 105**	**10 runners**				
AW FORM	NAME	BEST			LAST SIX			
7-210153	PAWN IN LIFE	109S08	101S08	109S08	94W09	100S08	90S08	101S07
42-2336	POINT OF DISPUTE	108L07	103W07	104L06	99L07	94W06	100L06	98W08
1-657977	WHAT-A-DANCER	108L07	94W06	106L10	89L10	94S07	94L08	102L07
698-6367	ARC EL CIEL	107S07	92W07	98W08	98S06	107S07	98S06	96S07
8184-585	STOIC LEADER	105W08	100W07	87W07	81W08	103L07	98L08	105W08
/534-80	THURLESTONE ROCK	105W06	102L07	100L06	100L06	99L07	98L06	97W06
1/2-7504	OUTER HEBRIDES	104L07	90W06	100L07	101L07	102L07	88S07	104L07
906-7861	MARKO JADEO	104L07	86L08	98W07	99L08	101L07	99L07	103W06
2337-	DISTANT COUNTRY	102W07			102W07	99W08	100W07	93W07

What-A-Dancer had some very smart form to his name over seven furlongs on Polytrack, so in theory he had conditions in his favour. Or at least he had smart form on the *Lingfield* Polytrack, so the question was whether he would be as well suited by *this* version of Polytrack. He hadn't shown a lot in two previous outings on this surface, but they had been over a different trip and I was happy to give him another chance, so I took £280-£40.

I soon found out the answer to my question. What-A-Dancer was held up in the early stages and in truth never offered a threat to the leaders. The race eventually went to Outer Hebrides, who had looked the biggest danger on my figures.

So I ended the day all-square, but should have done better. I played in more races than I should have done and paid the penalty.

Saturday 19 March – Lingfield

This meeting was the highlight of the All-Weather season, featuring two Listed races including the Littlewoods Bet Direct Winter Derby.

The first race on the card was a conditions event for unraced two-year-olds and I was happy to give the contest the swerve, but the second race was a very interesting conditions sprint.

2-25 BET DIRECT ON SKY ACTIVE SPRINT (CONDITIONS STAKES) (B1) 4YO+							
5 furlongs			Par = 109	10 runners			
AW FORM	NAME	BEST			LAST SIX		
/13541-1	DANCING MYSTERY	112L05	107S05	105L05	94L05	103S05	106S05	107S05
3105-649	ZARZU	110S05	99L05	94S05	101W05	100S05	101L05	99W05
8/4-5	DRAGON FLYER	109L05				88L05	109L05	104W05
5/320/1/	SMOKIN BEAU	108W05	98S05	98L06	99W06	97W05	87W05	108W05
526-2414	TREASURE CAY	108L06	105W05	108L06	107S05	102S05	102L05	105W05
22-12324	HIDDEN DRAGON	107W05	101L07	107S05	106S06	101L05	107W05	104W06
5621-323	MAGIC GLADE	106W05	99W05	102S05	105S05	106S05	106S05	106W05
	FAST HEART							
	IF PARADISE							
	SOCKS FOR GLENN							

The one I liked here was Treasure Cay. For well over a year horses starting from stall one had been having a wretched time of it with only three winners emerging from the inside draw since December 2003, but two of those victories had been by Treasure Cay himself and here he was in stall one yet again. For some reason being drawn right on the inside must have suited his style of running, so I talked myself into taking £320-£40.

Unfortunately things didn't work out for him this time, and it was left to the veteran Dancing Mystery to pip the outsider Fast Heart in a thrilling finish. In reality I had been rather too quick in dismissing Dancing Mystery's chances, because for some reason I had him down as more of a Southwell performer these days, but look at that 'best rating' column. His top figure had been earned here and making such a careless error of judgement meant I had missed an 8/1 winner.

I was determined to put things right quickly and an opportunity soon arose in the shape of the first Listed contest of the day.

3-00 BETDIRECT.CO.UK SPRING CUP (LISTED RACE) (A1) 3YO							
7 furlongs			Par = 106		11 runners		
AW FORM	NAME	BEST	LAST SIX				
31-111	PARTY BOSS	109W08		90W07	93S07	100W08	109W08	102L07
21	MOGAAMER	106L07					100L07	106L07
41-2	FRANCIS CADELL	102L06				81W07	98W06	102L06
-1352052	IL PRANZO	101L05	93L06	92W08	100L07	97L06	99W06	101L05
4-427313	GOLDHILL PRINCE	100L05	96L06	87L06	88W06	91L06	87L05	100L05
1-	SUMORA	96L05						96L05
211-	WATCHMYEYES	95W08				90L08	95W08	95W08
1-	TREMAR	95L06						95L06
0731-383	AGGRAVATION	93L07	85W07	90L07	93L06	93L07	90L07	91L06
	JUSTAQUESTION							
	GOLDEN LEGACY							

I had this down as a match between Party Boss, a horse I had really grown to like, and recent course winner Mogaamer. However, the favourite was Tremar, probably on account of him winning a Group Three race in France the previous autumn and also finishing sixth in the Dewhurst, but I wasn't that keen on him, as that figure of 95 for his course victory the previous year was going to need a good deal of improving on. I considered him to be a false favourite and was therefore happy to take £180-£40 about Party Boss and £140-£40 about Mogaamer.

To be fair, it did look for a long time as though Tremar might have stolen the race from the front, but eventually Party Boss hit top gear and got up to win comfortably from Francis Cadell, with Tremar fading into third and Mogaamer back in fourth.

I felt much happier now and was ready for the Winter Derby itself.

AW FORM	NAME	BEST	LAST SIX					
			3-30 LITTLEWOODS BET DIRECT WINTER DERBY (LISTED RACE) (A1) 4YO+					
			10 furlongs			Par = 111		14 runners
3021-	CORRIOLANUS	114L10			109L10	99L10	94L12	114L10
11/1	COUNSEL'S OPINION	113S12				101L12	113S12	109L10
/21-2234	COMPTON BOLTER	112L10	109L10	108W09	109L10	107W08	103L12	106L10
619-1121	ECCENTRIC	111L08	92L08	101L07	94L10	111L08	107L10	109L10
791-1252	MOAYED	110W08	104L06	109L07	110W08	106L06	101W08	99W07
/2/2191-	GRAND PASSION	110L10	98L07	108L10	103L10	110L10	100L10	110L10
2/13	HOWLE HILL	109L10				91L07	109L10	91L10
492-1521	GIG HARBOR	108L10	108L10	106W12	106L12	103L12	107L10	96W12
1-	CALUKI	103L10						103L10
31-	AFRICAN DREAM	102L08					97L08	102L08
	ECOMIUM							
	HURRICANE ALAN							
	BLYTHE KNIGHT							
	BILLY ALLEN							

A cracking renewal of the big race and several questions to be answered, but from my point of view there were only two important issues. Firstly, was the talking horse Ecomium going to prove as good as those around him seemed to think he was at the first time of asking on sand, and would Eccentric be allowed the soft lead that seemed vital to his chances?

I couldn't answer the first question, but I refused to believe that in a race of this quality no-one was going to serve it up to Eccentric early to try and test his suspect stamina. The pair I liked were Corriolanus, whose form was certainly good enough for a race like this and who was proven under the conditions, and Grand Passion who was better drawn than when a beaten favourite in this very race the previous year. So I happily took £480-£40 about Corriolanus and £400-£40 about Grand Passion.

As soon as the stalls opened I was horrified. John Egan bounced Eccentric out from stall one and was soon lobbing along in front with nothing keen to take him on for the early lead. Even at that stage the result had an air of inevitability about it and it was no surprise that Eccentric was able to kick off the final bend and quickly establish a race-winning lead.

As admirable as the winner was, I couldn't help thinking that his rivals had gifted him this victory.

Still, there was a fascinating and competitive handicap coming up, so I didn't dwell on spilt milk for too long.

4-05 BET DIRECT ON AT THE RACES INTERACTIVE HANDICAP (0-100) (C1) 4YO+								
7 furlongs			Par = 107			13 runners		
AW FORM	NAME	BEST	LAST SIX					
5410-740	LYGETON LAD	110L07	105L07	104L08	99L07	100W08	106L10	102W08
-6579776	WHAT-A-DANCER	108L07	106L10	89L10	94S07	94L08	102L07	92W07
2/03-22	RYDAL	108L06		95L07	95L07	108L06	105W06	105W06
123-1211	KATIYPOUR	107L10	104L08	105L10	96L07	105L07	106L06	105W06
103-R319	QUIET TIMES	107L06	92W06	102S05	0S05	104W06	107L06	101W06
952121-3	BINANTI	106L07	98L07	106L07	103W08	91L08	88L08	104L08
2/2123-	BAHIANO	106L07		96W07	95W08	103L07	102L08	106L07
1-	MASTER ROBBIE	106L07						106L07
11/67-	BRAVO MAESTRO	104L07			99L07	102L07	104L07	101L08
3/12-1	MR LAMBROS	103L07			103L06	102L07	102L07	103L07
2/73145-	JONNY EBENEEZER	98S06	93S07	79W07	97S07	91S06	98S06	97L06
	KILL CAT							

At first glance this race looked a minefield, but there were a couple of horses near the head of the market I was keen to take on and, with that pair out of the way, this race began to look a real opportunity. Kill Cat and Jonny Ebeneezer had been running well in Dubai, whilst Jonny Ebeneezer had also been one of the real success stories of the 2004 season, winning no less than eight times. However, there was no guarantee that Dubai form would work out on this surface and Jonny Ebeneezer had only won once from ten starts on sand, and that was at Southwell. Both horses were trading at around the 5/1 mark, but I couldn't have either of them. I could have laid them both on the betting exchanges, but I wanted to get more out of them than that so I decided to back a couple against them.

The field also included a few old friends from the previous week's sprint at Wolverhampton, including the first and second Katiypour and Rydal. Katiypour had to be included in my bets in his current mood despite being favourite, whilst Rydal had run so well from a bad draw at Wolverhampton that he had to be included too, even though there was some doubt about him getting the trip. Lygeton Lad had done me several favours over the years and even though he wasn't currently in the best of form, these were his ideal conditions and he looked sure to get the strong pace he requires. The last horse I wanted to include was Master Robbie, another to have been racing in Dubai, but a course-and-distance winner on his only previous try on sand in this country.

After what seemed like an endless trek around the bookmakers, I ended up with £160-£40 about Katiypour, £320-£40 about Rydal, £640-£40 about Lygeton Lad and £1000-£40 about Master Robbie.

The race couldn't have worked out better with Kill Cat and Jonny

Ebeneezer amongst the first beaten, and I watched with great joy and a small amount of disbelief as my four horses ran 1-2-3-4 with the biggest priced of the quartet Master Robbie leading them home.

As I packed the large wedge of banknotes into my wallet, I started to wonder why I hadn't also covered the four horses in combination exactas, the dividend of which was £307.80 to a £1 stake. It just goes to show that even after a big win you still have the right to criticise yourself for not making the profit even greater!

I was happy to sit out the next two races on the card, both maidens for older horses, but fired a double-barrelled salvo at the final contest.

5-35 BET DIRECT ON AT THE RACES HANDICAP (0-85) (D2) 4YO+							
8 furlongs				Par = 105		12 runners	
AW FORM	NAME	BEST			LAST SIX		
1201-022	RED CONTACT	112S08	106S08	94L10	107S08	98W08	104S07	112S08
92-05313	ANUVASTEEL	106W08	103W09	93L10	104L10	103L10	106W08	101W08
2/45-9	OUR TEDDY	106L10			106L07	100L08	106L10	97L08
/1195-48	DANCE ON THE TOP	106L08	106L08	103L08	100L07	100L08	103L08	92L10
553-0617	STEELY DAN	106L07	106L07	87L08	97L07	94L08	105L07	105L10
11/4-220	TAKES TUTU	106L07	91S07	106L07	97L07	103L07	95L07	100L07
289	TEDSTALE	105W09				105W09	94L08	104W08
1180-655	CHEROKEE NATION	105L06	105L06	99L06	90L06	102L07	94L08	101W06
565-2217	KABEER	104L10	96L07	94L07	104L10	102L10	101L08	102L10
7634/22-	BLUE TROJAN	101L10	79W09	100W08	100L08	99L10	101L10	94L10
104-	ADMIRAL COMPTON	101L07				100L08	101L07	89L08
	DAFORE							

One of those near the top of the market, and top on my figures, was Red Contact, but he was just the type of transparent performer that I love. His form figures on Fibresand were 12122, whilst his figures on Polytrack read 97400. No prizes for guessing that I considered him to be the lay of the day, even more so than Kill Cat and Jonny Ebeneezer!

The pair I liked were Dance On the Top and Steely Dan, both proven performers on the surface, so I took £480-£40 about the former and £280-£40 about the latter.

As things turned out, neither of my selections managed to figure in the finish though Dance On The Top did show up for a long way. The race went to Kabeer, who managed to gain an uncontested lead and kept more than enough in reserve for the business end, in a similar vein to Eccentric.

Incidentally, Red Contact only managed to beat two horses home.

Saturday 2 April – Wolverhampton

The Saturday evening meetings at Wolverhampton are a joy to attend and especially so this time as it was 'A Tribute To Blondie' night, an occasion that took me back to my youth when I had Debbie Harry on my bedroom wall, but that's another story.

There didn't look to be that many decent betting opportunities on the card, but I felt I had spotted one in the opening claimer as there were only three horses in it as far as I was concerned.

7-00 TROTTY'S 50TH BIRTHDAY CLAIMING STAKES (6) 4YO+								
6 furlongs				Par = 101		10 runners		
AW FORM	**NAME**	**BEST**			**LAST SIX**			
441F-775	GILDED COVE	108W05	101S06	95W05	0W05	88S06	93W06	102L06
4-172523	OLD BAILEY	105S06	105S06	92W07	102S06	96S06	101S07	94S06
21436-31	SAMUEL CHARLES	104W07	104W07	92W07	99W07	95W07	98W07	102L07
58-82942	DVINSKY	103W07	95W07	96L08	103W07	93W08	96W07	102L06
108-5747	PANJANDRUM	103L05	89W05	84W06	94L05	98L06	96W05	92L06
9-588432	ST IVIAN	102S06	100S06	87W06	93S06	98S06	98S07	94S06
/7P9/57-	ONLY FOR GOLD	99W07	94W08	87W09	0W09	73W07	89W05	90S07
0/044/02	GEORGE ROMNEY	98L08	90L12	52W08	98L08	96W08	71W12	95L07
07959-80	ELLAMYTE	88L06	74W09	81L05	82W07	77W07	84W05	58S08

Gilded Cove was certainly one of them, but he hadn't been in the best of form since the turn of the year. Samuel Charles had scored at Lingfield the previous day and even though he was a contender on the ratings, this trip seemed likely to be too sharp for him. That left Dvinsky, who had shown in his previous start at Lingfield that the drop back to six furlongs was not a problem for him. He was also better drawn than the other pair in stall two, so even though odds of 5/2 were shorter than I hoped for, I waded in to take £100-£40.

The race didn't exactly pan out as I would have wished. Dvinsky seemed to be in the ideal position to strike on the inside of the field turning for home, but didn't pick up at all and ended up a never-nearer fifth. The other pair on my shortlist ultimately fought out the finish, with the one-eyed Gilded Cove getting the better of Samuel Charles by half a length. The winner's starting price was 11/2 and in reality I should have backed all three contenders, as their respective prices just about justified it and I couldn't see the winner coming from anywhere else.

The next race on the card was a two-year-old seller with only four runners, so no bet there, and the horse I had intended backing in the next race was withdrawn after a particularly grotesque incident in which the assistant trainer of my selection was badly injured by another horse in the paddock.

The next race was a maiden for older horses and with little form to go on and nothing outstanding on the figures, my second bet didn't occur until the fifth race on the card, a handicap over the extended mile.

9-00 DINE IN THE ZONGALERO HANDICAP (0-70) (5) 3YO+								
8.6 furlongs			Par = 103			9 runners		
AW FORM	NAME	BEST	LAST SIX					
64115321	SORBIESHARRY	106W09	105W08	103W09	106W09	97W08	103S12	105W08
521-3724	KING NICHOLAS	105W08	102W08	102S08	101W08	85S08	105W08	97W09
/351-112	CHERISHED NUMBER	105W08	94W08	97W09	99W08	105W08	102W08	103W08
4/70-423	LOCKSTOCK	104W08	100S08	90S08	77L10	104W08	99W07	97W07
-3341322	BALLYGRIFFIN KID	104S08	96W07	102W08	102L08	98W07	104S08	98L10
4820-654	ACORAZADO	104L08	97L07	101L07	94L07	85L06	100W08	98W09
80-1U18	WILTSHIRE	101L08	70S07	86L07	95W07	0L07	101L08	95L08
U5/152-5	ALWAYS FLYING	98S12	0W06	93W08	98W09	91L10	98S12	92W12
57	DISCOMANIA	94W08					94W08	87L12

This race was almost a carbon copy of the first contest with just the three possible contenders in my opinion, but just to show that it is possible to make the same mistake twice in one night, I again missed out on a winner by sticking pig-headedly to my opinion despite the evidence right in front of my eyes.

Sorbiesharry looked an obvious selection, almost too obvious, and because of that I was convinced he was going to start at less than 2/1 and therefore too short for a race like this. I liked Cherished Number, but settled on King Nicholas as he was starting from stall two and that box was enjoying a lot of success just now. I really should have paid more attention to Sorbiesharry's price rather than narrow-mindedly trying to get £240-£40 about King Nicholas.

Almost inevitably, Sorbiesharry won and how I let him go off unbacked at odds of around 7/2 I'll never know.

Bloodied but not demoralised, I was looking forward to the last race as I thought this was a great opportunity to end the evening with a bang.

9-30 HOLIDAY INN DUNSTALL PARK HANDICAP (0-70) (5) 3YO+							
7.1 furlongs				Par = 103		11 runners	
AW FORM	NAME	BEST	LAST SIX				
9-111121	FRATERNITY	106L12	98W08	103S08	100W08	99W06	100S08	103W08
2351-336	BIJOU DAN	103W07	97S08	92W09	102W08	101W08	103W07	95W08
-1487752	MERDIFF	102S07	94W07	90W07	94W07	100S05	95W07	99W07
879-2538	ZAFARSHAH	102L07	92W08	87W07	94W07	94L08	97W08	93W08
40229-01	LORD CHAMBERLAIN	99W08	95L07	98W07	99W08	83S08	90W09	85W08
6-0886	HOH BLEU DEE	96L06		96L06	94L07	93W07	94W08	95W07
4/009-90	MARSHALLSPARK	95W05	84S06	95W05	86W06	86W07	81S06	92S07
07/5227-	BEN KENOBI	93W07	57W09	75W09	85W07	93W07	90W09	76W12
9-	FULL SPATE	89W06						89W06
0	PENDING	83W09						83W09

Fraternity was going to be all the rage in his current mood and was therefore going to be a very short price. I was right about that and really wanted to take him on. Most of his success had been in banded company, but he had stepped up to win in similar grade to this last time, so class wasn't necessarily the problem. He was also a front-runner and with no other obvious tearaways in the line-up, it did seem as though he was going to enjoy as uncontested lead. The problem was that he had been dominating his rivals over longer trips and they would be going that much faster over this shorter distance, so he could find trying to make every yard that much more difficult.

The one I chose to take advantage was Bijou Dan, who was competitive on the figures and proven over the trip. The only problem was he was drawn wide in stall ten, but even with that negative I was more than happy to take £280-£40.

My feeling about Fraternity was proved absolutely right, because although he managed to lead early he could never get clear of these speedier types and was headed and beaten on the home turn. Bijou Dan had been the one to serve it up to the favourite before halfway and soon forged his way into an advantage of a couple of lengths starting up the home straight, but my fears about the draw then came to fruition. Bijou Dan had done a lot of running early on from his wide draw in order to take a prominent position, and those exertions eventually told in the latter stages. Rolling about under pressure as he began to tire, he did his best to hold on but the 12-year-old Lord Chamberlain had managed to conserve enough energy for the latter stages of the race to run him out of it.

Close, but no cigar.

Saturday 9 April – Lingfield

Whilst the eyes of the racing world were fixed firmly on the Aintree Grand National, I was aiming myself towards Lingfield. A huge crowd turned up as well which surprised me a bit, but at least that meant that the betting market should be strong.

The first race on the card was a two-year-old maiden, not normally my favourite type of contest at this time of year with usually so little sand form to go on, but this race turned out to be a little bit different.

2-00 BETDIRECT.CO.UK MAIDEN AUCTION STAKES (5) 2YO								
5 furlongs					Par = 92		7 runners	
AW FORM	NAME	BEST			LAST SIX			
2	PICCOSTAR	90L05						90L05
3	KUNG HEI	81L05						81L05
4	CASABLANCA MINX	78L05						78L05
	GETBUZZIN							
	CROCODILE BAY							
	HASTY PASSION							
	DREAM FACTOR							

I considered Piccostar to be the most likely winner, not just because she had already performed very well here on her racecourse debut, but also because she had a lovely draw in stall two from which to make her experience count. The problem was that she seemed certain to start short enough in the market and duly opened at 13/8, which wasn't really the sort of price I wanted to get involved at. However, a gamble started to develop on Jamie Osborne's newcomer Crocodile Bay, which resulted in Piccostar drifting right out to 9/4. I had to have a bit of that so I enthusiastically took £90-£40 about her.

Once the race was under way, I never had a moment's worry. Piccostar bounced out of the gate and ran her rivals into the ground. It has become a bit of a cliché, but if only all races were always as straightforward as this one.

The second contest on the card was a valuable Listed event over a mile in which only one of the five runners had previously run on sand. Races like this can be great betting opportunities as I have said before, and in this instance the four sand newcomers were taking on none other than our old friend Party Boss, winner of a Listed contest at this track the previous month and probably one of the top All-Weather horses of the entire winter. Unfortunately, the betting public had come to the same conclusion as I had and I wasn't prepared to get involved at the sort of skinny price on offer about him. Instead I was more than happy just to see him win, which he duly did with consummate ease.

I had to get involved in the third race though.

3-05 PRESS RED TO BET ON ITV HANDICAP (0-70) (5) 3YO+								
8 furlongs			Par = 103			8 runners		
AW FORM	NAME	BEST	LAST SIX					
407/0644	DIAMOND MAX	105W08	75W08	98W08	98L07	101L06	97S07	102L08
29-24512	MOLINIA	104W08	92S08	103S07	101S07	96S07	93W08	102S08
33413224	BALLYGRIFFIN KID	104S08	102W08	102L08	98W07	104S08	98L10	101W08
820-6542	ACORAZADO	104L08	101L07	94L07	85L06	100W08	98W09	103W08
76-	RUSSIAN APPLAUSE	98L07					82S08	98L07
32/537-	PHLUKE	95L06		90S07	95L06	94L07	94S07	91L07
8-	IN DREAM'S	86L07						86L07
	BLAEBERRY							

I narrowed this race down to just two contenders after firstly eliminating Molinia on account of her lack of form at the track, and then kicking Acorazado into touch as he seemed most unlikely to get the true pace he needs. I did like Ballygriffin Kid, but preferred Diamond Max that bit more. In his last outing over this course and distance, he had suggested that he was just about to run into form so I happily took £160-£40 about him, but as things turned out he ran a very listless race and could manage only fifth. On the positive side I was right about both Molinia and Acorazado, but never really considered the eventual winner Phluke who must have improved quite a bit after a seven-month break.

The fourth race on the card was an intriguing conditions event and included one or two old friends.

3-40 LITTLEWOODS BET DIRECT CONDITIONS STAKES (4) 4YO+								
7 furlongs			Par = 105		6 runners			
AW FORM	NAME	BEST	LAST SIX					
111110-2	VORTEX	114W08	98L08	104W08	101W08	114W08	97L10	110W08
410-7402	LYGETON LAD	110L07	104L08	99L07	100W08	106L10	102W08	107L07
159	PRINCE TUM TUM	106W06				106W06	103L06	103W08
2/2123-5	BAHIANO	106L07	96W07	95W08	103L07	102L08	106L07	104L07
	PSYCHIATRIST							
	CAPE FEAR							

The forecast favourite was Vortex and I'm sure you will remember that he had run such a massive race in the Lincoln Trial at Wolverhampton the previous month, before finishing a fine fifth in the big Doncaster contest itself. I was happy to take him on though, and for two very good reasons. Firstly, he was returning to the track just a week after his hard race in the Lincoln and, probably more importantly, although he had won on this track in the past his very best sand form was achieved elsewhere. Also, this looked as though it might turn into something of a tactical race, so I preferred to take £280-£40 about his stable-companion Lygeton Lad, who was racing under his optimum conditions and who had run so well in that handicap won by Master Robbie here the previous month.

I must admit at one stage I was quite happy with myself as it seemed that Vortex was in a spot of bother, but that feeling didn't last long as he seemed to get stronger as the race progressed and, in the end, won with a degree of comfort. Perhaps Vortex's starting price of 3/1 wasn't so bad after all considering his advantage on my speed figures. As for Lygeton Lad, he never really threatened and could finish only fifth.

The penultimate race on the card was the sort of race I normally shy away from on sand, a three-year-old maiden.

4-30 BET DIRECT ON SKY ACTIVE MAIDEN STAKES (5) 3YO								
6 furlongs			Par = 98			11 runners		
AW FORM	NAME	BEST	LAST SIX					
43-4	MOON BIRD	95L06				95L06	93W06	88L06
32044-	GAUDALPIN	94W05		85L05	88W06	75W05	94W05	91W06
073-	GIRLSWEEKEND	94L06				71L06	84L07	94L06
026	CAYMAN COLONY	91L07	81L07	91L07	90L07			
6	WINDERMERE ISLAND	84L06						84L06
	HAYYANI							
	GRAMADA							
	SHRINE MOUNTAIN							
	PICKAPEPPA							
	MY DREAM							
	SCUBA							

However, I decided that this was too good an opportunity to miss, as I didn't like the look of two of those near the head of the market. One was Cayman Colony, who had a bit to find on my figures and I'm sure owed his position in the betting to coming from a big yard. The other main contender according to the market was the newcomer Hayyani, who was only so prominent in the market because he held an entry in the 2000 Guineas.

I had to take them both on and decided to back two against them. The first one I decided to side with was Moon Bird, who had run well enough on this track in the past to be worthy of support and was also top on my figures, whilst at a much longer price was Girlsweekend, whose profile had a progressive look to it and the only reason she was such a big price was that she came from an unfashionable stable. I wasn't so bothered about that, though the four-month absence was a slight concern, but even so I was more than happy to take £200-£40 about Moon Bird and £640-£40 about Girlsweekend.

I was starting to get quite excited as the field hit the home straight as Girlsweekend had moved to the front and was making the best of her way home. It seemed as though I was going to pick up a nice payoff, but whether it was lack of a recent outing or something else, her stride then began to shorten and she was mugged near the line by a couple of rivals. One of them was Hayyani, who did at least demonstrate some ability, but fortunately for me the other one was Moon Bird who just got up to beat them both.

It would have been nicer had Girlsweekend won, but the logic in my thinking was proved correct and a profit was made.

The last race on the card was perhaps the most competitive of the afternoon.

5-00 PLAY GAMEON ON ITV FILLIES' HANDICAP (0-60) (6) 3YO+							
8 furlongs			Par = 98		12 runners		
AW FORM	NAME	BEST	LAST SIX				
00-68182	MY LILLI	105L10	85L10	95L08	98L10	95L07	91L08	105L10
532013-8	RYAN'S BLISS	101L10	94L10	99L10	87L10	101L10	95L08	93L08
5-952144	ROWAN PURSUIT	101L08	90L08	96L07	92L08	101L08	92L08	98L10
9289-00	HOT LIPS PAGE	101L08	83L08	101L08	90W09	77W08	85L07	89L07
62521514	VIZULIZE	98L10	97L10	92W09	96W09	98L10	89W08	95W08
015751-6	LITTLETON ZEPHIR	98L08	94L08	88S07	91S08	96L08	95L08	92L08
0-9912	JAHIA	96L08		89L10	92L07	87L08	96L07	96L08
8	AVERLLINE	92L08						92L08
70/90008	IPHIGENIA	92L07	0S07	71W07	86L07	92L07	85L08	90L08
84-00	EMPIRE OF THE SUN	89W07			89W07	89W07	84L08	87W07
0-7	MAJESTIC STAR	85L08					70L10	85L08
8	BUZZ BUZZ	68S08						68S08

There were only three contenders as far as I could see, namely My Lilli, Rowan Pursuit and Littleton Zephir. Unfortunately they were also the first three in the market, which made backing all of them unattractive, so I forced myself into taking a singular view. Big Mistake!

I was concerned that My Lilli's best recent efforts had been over different trips to today's, so rejected her on those grounds. Littleton Zephir was a real eye-catcher in her most recent start at this track and indeed I had written the Raceform Notebook for that very meeting. What I had actually said about her was:

'Littleton Zephir, returning from a three-month break having been withdrawn with a vet's certificate from two intended outings in the meantime, had an absolute nightmare. Despite always being within a couple of lengths of the leaders, she never saw any delight at all and her rider just had to sit and suffer all the way down the home straight. How she would have fared had she got out is anyone's guess, but she is definitely one to keep a close eye on.'

Yet somehow I still didn't back her in this race. I must admit I do have a problem backing supposedly unlucky horses next time out when they are near the head of the market, as I always think the betting public overreact to a horse being 'unlucky', but that really is no excuse. Instead I took £200-£40 about Rowan Pursuit who looked much more solid to me, but of course as things turned out Littleton Zephir bolted up by five lengths from Rowan Pursuit, with My Lilli back in third.

A profitable day, but it really should have been an awful lot better.

Friday 27 May – Wolverhampton

A combination of work commitments, and fewer meetings on sand as the spring continued, meant that it was a little while before I was able to attend my next All-Weather meeting. I had hoped to attend a few meetings at Southwell during June to give a nice balance between the Polytrack and Fibresand venues in the diary, but that project had to be knocked on the head when I found out that Southwell was closing down whilst they built a new weighing room, and its meetings transferred to Wolverhampton. It was unlikely the track would reopen before the period of the diary was due to end either, so I had to be content with just the two Polytrack courses for now.

The opportunity to attend this Wolverhampton meeting came rather unexpectedly, so I was particularly determined to make the most of it.

The first thing to mention about this meeting was how hot it was, in fact in many parts of the country it was the hottest May day for 50 years and there I was prancing around Dunstall Park in a suit!

Quite part from how much fluid I was losing, my main concern was whether these hot, dry conditions would affect the way the track rode. By this stage of the year I had some pretty firm views on the effects of the draw, pace biases, etc., but my statistics had all been established from meetings outside the summer period and the question was whether the status quo would be maintained, or would the track conditions be turned on their head in the current climate? Only when a few races had been run could I begin to answer these questions.

As things turned out I was going to be able to observe the first race on the card, the one-mile seller, without any financial interest as my original choice Blue Empire was announced as a non-runner and I didn't fancy anything else in the race.

The second race on the card was a different matter. Here, I felt, was a decent betting opportunity.

3-00 STEVE EVANS OF ALTON LODGE HOTEL, CHESTER HANDICAP (0-60) (6) 3YO+							
9.5 furlongs		Par = 101	13 runners				
AW FORM	NAME	BEST	LAST SIX				
2703600-	YORKER	104S07	86W08	91W07	95S08	90S07	89W07	91W09
070-7695	SEWMORE CHARACTER	103L10	91W08	90W09	95W08	97W09	93W12	90L08
0368-300	RED SKELTON	102L10	98W09	95W08	71W09	98W09	91W12	80W09
638-0001	WANNA SHOUT	102L08	94W09	88W08	89L08	88W08	90W08	100W08
/7/3/64/	SUMMER BOUNTY	100W09	98W12	92L13	82W09	97W08	89W12	100W09
87-703	KING AT LAST	100W08		88L08	91L07	92L08	97L08	100W08
23-56231	FARNBOROUGH	100L10	95S12	93W09	95S14	99W09	100L10	98W08
77331520	PEACE EMBLEM	99W09	94W09	99W08	99W09	95W12	98W12	85W09
6-088646	HOH BLEU DEE	99W07	94L07	93W07	94W08	95W07	99W07	88W09
211-2	KINGS TOPIC	99L10			96L10	96L10	99L10	90W09
004	BARRISSIMO	96L08				81S08	86L08	96L08
0-	DANETTIE	76W07						76W07

The forecast favourite was Summer Bounty, who on my ratings had only an average chance at best. He had never run on Polytrack in his life and was racing on sand for the first time in well over two years. Why was he so short in the market then? Well the 'lbs and lengths' merchants were getting very excited because he was racing off a 20lb lower mark than on turf, and if you add in the 'Frankie (Dettori) Factor', then you begin to see why.

Perhaps I'm being naïve, but if an experienced horse is rated significantly higher on one surface than another then I believe there is an obvious and valid reason for that, i.e. they aren't so good on the other surface. I had no reason to believe that Summer Bounty was an improved performer since finishing fourth of eight off a mark of just 48 (8lb lower than today's) on the old Fibresand surface here in February 2003, so he just had to be taken on.

The pair I liked were Farnborough, who had solid course form and had won here last time out, and King At Last, a lightly raced sort who had put up his best-ever performance here last time, and whom I believed would relish today's longer trip. I therefore took £160-£40 about Farnborough and £440-£40 about King At Last.

As things turned out, King At Last raced in the ideal position just behind the leader, but found nothing off the bride once into the home straight, which was disappointing considering how well he had travelled up to that point.

Farnborough, on the other hand, was given quite a bit to do but his biggest problem was that he was brought widest of all rounding the home bend. As I have said before, you can't afford to do that at Wolverhampton these days unless you have a ton in hand of your rivals. The gelding was still a couple of lengths adrift of the winner Kings Topic at the line, but would have been much closer had he taken more of an inside route. Still, this did rather suggest that the weather conditions had not created a different track bias and things appeared to be as normal.

As for Summer Bounty, he only beat two home though he did have an excuse as he finished lame. In fact this contest was noteworthy for its number of sick and wounded judging by the official explanations. Quite apart from Summer Bounty, Red Skelton had hung right throughout, Sewmore Character had a breathing problem and Barrissimo coughed after the race!

The third contest on the card was a pretty bad three-year-old claimer and I shouldn't have got involved. The only reason I did was that this trip was going to be a new experience for several of the runners, on sand at least, and I might get an edge that way.

3-30	THE ZONGALERO RESTAURANT AT DUNSTALL PARK CLAIMING STAKES (6) 3YO							
12.2 furlongs			Par = 97	7 runners				
AW FORM	NAME	BEST	LAST SIX					
0407-245	FERRARA FLAME	99S11	88W09	73W08	88W08	95W08	99S11	94S12
9316-342	SONNTAG BLUE	96S08	96S08	93W08	91S08	95L08	90S08	83S08
071-366	BELLALOU	94W09	66L07	88S08	92L08	90W09	94W09	93W08
496143	JOSEAR	94S12	90W09	88L08	90S08	92S08	93W09	94S12
9	JOEY	93W09		93W09				
	GOODENOUGH BLUE							
	OLIVIA TWIST							

Only two in this field had attempted this far on sand before, yet the favourite Sonntag Blue was stepping up half a mile in trip and had a speedy pedigree, so he was surely another one to take on.

I preferred Ferrara Flame over Josear, not just because of the higher rating, but I could just imagine him being given a typical George Baker waiting ride in the first-time visor before picking off the non-stayers late on. He started to drift in the market just before the off as the money came for Josear, but that didn't stop me from taking £160-£40 about him.

I was right about Ferrara Flame being held up right out the back, but unfortunately his late effort was laboured to say the least and he never threatened to get any closer than fourth behind the winner Bellalou.

If getting involved in the claimer had been a mistake, the next race on the card was a gilt-edged opportunity which I had been very much looking forward to.

4-00	EUROPEAN BREEDERS FUND MAIDEN STAKES (5) 2YO							
6 furlongs			Par = 93	9 runners				
AW FORM	NAME	BEST	LAST SIX					
3	BRENDA MEOVA	92W05						92W05
	STRATHAM							
	HIGH COMMAND							
	LITTLE MISS DAISY							
	EGYPTIAN LORD							
	CHARLLEN							
	HILL OF HOWTH							
	BUZZIN'BOYZEE							
	INDIAN WIZARD							

At first glance this may not be the sort of race that appeals as a major betting opportunity. After all, only one of the nine runners had raced on sand before and there were several unknown quantities in the line-up, but having delved a bit deeper a wonderful opportunity began to surface.

Hill Of Howth was forecast to go off at odds-on (which he eventually did) on account of finishing second to an Aidan O'Brien juvenile on his York debut. Quite apart from the perceived drop in class, the fact that he was beaten by a Ballydoyle inmate made the form look especially strong, or so it seemed. A closer look at the York race showed that the winning time was very ordinary and there was always the question as to how he would cope with this different surface. Those doubts made his starting price of 8/11 look distinctly fragile.

Brenda Meova, on the other hand, had run perfectly well on this surface on her second outing (notice how close the figure she earned for that performance is to the par for this race) and a couple of subsequent winners had already come out of that contest. She had run well back on turf since then too and was also well drawn here, so with all of those factors in her favour she just had to be backed at 8/1. Rarely have I struck a bet of £320-£40 with such confidence.

The first point to be made about this race once the stalls opened was that the favourite hardly went a yard and eventually ended up a well-beaten sixth. That's not to say it left the race at the mercy of Brenda Meova though. Stratham looked to have established an unassailable lead a furlong out, but fortunately for me he then wilted completely and my selection got up to win by a length from the fast-finishing High Command with Stratham a short head away in third.

This was a race where a little bit of time and effort had resulted in drawing conclusions which proved spot-on, and there's something especially satisfying about picking up your winnings after a contest like this.

With the money now safely tucked away, I looked forward to the following sprint handicap with increased enthusiasm, as this was another race in which I had a confident selection.

4-30 BURMATEX INFINITY HANDICAP (0-70) (5) 3YO+								
6 furlongs			Par = 103	13 runners				
AW FORM	NAME	BEST	LAST SIX					
53/0100-	MISTER MAL	109W07	94S07	86W06	81W07	102S06	85W05	87S06
/0446-90	PADDYWACK	109W05	63S06	102W05	98W06	96W06	96L06	95W05
F-775141	GILDED COVE	108W05	88S06	93W06	102L06	101W06	99W05	105S05
42/6-422	KARMINSKEY PARK	107L05	101S05	102L05	92W06	97W05	104L06	96W06
1510-217	TURN AROUND	106S07	88W07	106S07	84S06	94W08	100S06	84W07
924-4865	BLYTHE SPIRIT	105W06	105W06	98W06	100S05	100L06	99W05	95L05
421-1035	CASHEL MEAD	105S06	99W06	104S05	96W05	91W05	98W06	99S05

555-5211	LOUISIADE	103W07	90S07	94S08	88S06	95W07	97W07	103W07
7-240520	ADANTINO	103L07	98W06	100L05	89L07	95W07	102L06	92L06
32/0591-	NO GROUSE	100W07	87W08	94W09	96S07	99W08	92W07	100W07
	LETS GET IT ON							
	GEORGE THE BEST							

The only problem was that everyone else seemed to have come to the same conclusion that Louisiade was a solid bet, as all the pundits made him their selection. It was perfectly understandable though, because the horse had been in fine form and was starting from the hugely advantaged number one stall. The only question mark against him as far as I was concerned was that his best recent efforts on sand had come over seven furlongs, and would he therefore be able to hold his position from the inside gate over this trip. Even the fact that he had won over this distance on turf last time out was no guarantee, given the different nature of the tracks. I should also have made his skinny price of 3/1 a negative in a race like this, but I was playing with winnings, so I got greedy and took £120-£40.

To be fair, even though Louisiade had to be niggled along to hold his place down the back straight, he was in the perfect position on the inside turning in but was just not quite good enough. Adantino, a horse I never seemed to catch right, got up right on the line to beat Turn Around with Louisiade close behind in third.

The last race on the card was a fillies' handicap and I probably should have left before it. Races like this have never been my speciality, but I thought I had found a bet.

5-00 PROFESSIONAL SERVICES FILLIES' HANDICAP (0-60) (6) 3YO+								
7.1 furlongs			Par = 98	12 runners				
AW FORM	NAME	BEST			LAST SIX			
04860313	BLAKESHALL QUEST	111W05	80S07	90S06	73W07	96S06	100S06	98S07
00631462	SPARK UP	104W08	93W07	94W07	97W07	91W06	99W08	92W07
96-50093	SWEETEST REVENGE	104L06	86W06	100L06	88L07	94L06	100L06	94W06
9-814628	EPITOMISE	95W07	89W07	92S07	95W07	87L07	94L07	90L07
399	SIERRA	95W07				95W07	91L08	90W08
31460-	MISKINA	94W07		93W08	94W07	94W07	92W08	86W07
02	TINTAC	92L08					92W09	92L08
927-200	SWEET PICKLE	92L07	85W05	92L07	91L06	89L07	86W06	85L07
5-087	AZEEZAH	91S06			91W07	85W09	81W09	91S06
	NEFERURA							

These were Spark Up's ideal conditions and with question marks over those at the head of the market, despite a less-than-favourable draw a bet of £240-£40 about the mare looked fully justified.

Spark Up ran her race and nearly got up to finish third, but as I said before races like this are not really my cup of tea as these fillies and mares seem to be very inconsistent. I can't really use the draw as an excuse for Spark Up's defeat either, as the first two home, Sweet Pickle and Sweetest Revenge, came from even wider draws.

So once again this was a winning day even if it was down to just one horse, but at least it demonstrates the value to be had when you can identify a vulnerable short-priced favourite, a sentiment that applies to all types of racing, not just on sand.

Saturday 9 July – Lingfield

This meeting was very special to me on a personal level. I had dreamt of the day when a Group race would be run on sand and that day had now come. Admittedly the only reason the race in question was being staged at Lingfield was because the fixture had been transferred from Ascot whilst the Berkshire track was being renovated, but it appeared that Ladbrokes (who were sponsoring the whole card) had asked the BHB if the entire meeting could be run on the Polytrack. Perhaps they were conscious of the fact that the field sizes would stand up better, especially for the big race, if the meeting was held on a consistent and forgiving surface rather than on the fast ground that was currently prevalent on turf.

As luck would have it, my two-week holiday in Scotland had come to an end the previous day and even though my dear wife had done all the driving on our vacation, I still felt a little bit jaded just 18 hours after the near 400-mile drive back down from Perth. At this stage of proceedings I had no reason to believe that post-holiday syndrome combined with my rather rushed preparation would have any effect on my judgement. I certainly felt confident enough as the time approached for the first race on the card, a rather tasty five-furlong handicap.

1-00 LADBROKES.COM HANDICAP (0-105) (2) 3YO+							
5 furlongs		Par = 109	10 runners				
AW FORM	NAME	BEST	LAST SIX				
13541-11	DANCING MYSTERY	112L05	105L05	94L05	103S05	106S05	107S05	102L05
/320/1/4	SMOKIN BEAU	108W05	98L06	99W06	97W05	87W05	108W05	99L05
2113/10-	TEXAS GOLD	107L06	103L05	104L06	107L06	107L06	102L05	89W06
561121-4	FOREVER PHOENIX	105S05	91L06	102S06	101L06	105L06	105L05	105S05
1-5	SUMORA	101L07					96L05	101L07
2	FAST HEART	101L05						101L05
11-	BOND CITY	98W05					98W05	94L05
	CORNUS							
	CAPE ROYAL							
	NIGHT PROSPECTOR							

At least it looked tasty beforehand, especially as by my reckoning several of those near the head of the market had questions to answer. Texas Gold looked possibly better suited by six furlongs on sand, whilst Bond City, despite his unbeaten record on artificial surfaces, was going to have to improve significantly on his previous sand form to figure. My eye was drawn to both the top two on my ratings, namely Dancing Mystery and Smokin Beau, despite their combined age of 19 years. Quite why I didn't back them both God only knows, but for some reason I was completely dazzled by the 16/1 freely available on old Dancing Mystery and enthusiastically took £640-£40 about him, whilst leaving Smokin Beau completely unbacked. Naturally I got what I deserved as Smokin Beau romped home at 8/1, whilst Dancing Mystery finished a never-nearer seventh.

It's a strange thing about five-furlong races on the Lingfield Polytrack, but quite often they aren't particular strongly run like you would expect and this contest was another example. Perhaps the fact that the field have to race around two bends in a short space of time, with the first one coming after just half a furlong, forces the runners to take things steadily in order to negotiate the bends properly. Whatever the reason, you often find that due to the modest pace the horses finish in a bit of a heap and those held up for a late run are never able to land an effective blow. In this particular race, a little over three lengths separated the first eight horses.

The second race on the card couldn't have been more of a contrast to the first. This was a £50,000 handicap over two miles and not surprisingly it attracted a decent field.

1-30 LADBROKESPOKER.COM STAKES (HERITAGE HANDICAP) (0-105) (2) 3YO+							
16 furlongs			**Par = 109**		**13 runners**		
AW FORM	NAME	BEST	LAST SIX				
5-131242	COLD TURKEY	113L12	113L12	105L12	105L12	95W12	98L13	103L16
03-44	SALUTE	112L12			89W09	108L10	112L12	93L12
92-15210	GIG HARBOR	112L10	106W12	106L12	103L12	107L10	96W12	112L10
2/130	HOWLE HILL	109L10			91L07	109L10	91L10	105L10
02/1	ODIHAM	106L16				80L07	96L08	106L16
/0772-85	HIGH POINT	105L16	93L12	92L12	96L12	105L16	97L12	101L16
0/52/18-	MAMCAZMA	102S11	96S08	73S08	102S12	102S11	98W16	92L12
0/31-	PEAK OF PERFECTION	100W08				87L08	100W08	98L12
11-	GOLDEN QUEST	96L12					95W12	96L12
50/	INCHPAST	90L08					90L08	78S07
	CORRIB ECLIPSE							
	HIGH ACTION							
	SWIFT SAILOR							

Ever since he had beaten Cold Turkey easily over this course and distance back in May, I had made a mental note to back Odiham if he turned out for this, and here he was. I particularly liked his chances because there were so few proven sand stayers in the field. Several in this line up had decent form over shorter on sand, whilst others stayed the trip well enough on turf, but Odiham had already proved himself under these conditions. He was a longer price than I had expected too, mainly because the public had for some reason backed Peak Of Perfection down to favouritism, but he was a front-runner and my statistics showed that front-runners had an abysmal record over staying trips on this track. So I was more than happy to take £200-£40 about Odiham and considered the Mark Johnston pair of Golden Quest and Swift Sailor much bigger dangers to my selection than the favourite.

The race went more or less as I had expected. Peak Of Perfection made the running for a mile and a half before falling in a heap, but unfortunately Odiham came off the bridle at around the same time and I was soon getting that sinking feeling. The race eventually went to sand-debutant High Action, with the Johnston pair Golden Quest and Swift Sailor filling second and third. Odiham had responded to pressure to finish a respectable fourth, but that was little compensation as I waved goodbye to another £40.

It was now time for the big race and for history to be made.

2-00 LADBROKES SILVER TROPHY STAKES (GROUP 3) (1) 4YO+							
8 furlongs			Par = 113		12 runners		
AW FORM	NAME	BEST	LAST SIX				
19-11211	ECCENTRIC	116L10	101L07	94L10	111L08	107L10	109L10	116L10
11110-21	VORTEX	114W08	104W08	101W08	114W08	97L10	110W08	111L07
10-74025	LYGETON LAD	110L07	99L07	100W08	106L10	102W08	107L07	106L07
21/14-	JACK SULLIVAN	109L07			101L07	96L07	109L07	102L08
/2123-54	BAHIANO	107L07	95W08	103L07	102L08	106L07	104L07	107L07
9/	BABODANA	101L10		101L10				
	AUTUMN GLORY							
	PENTECOST							
	AKIMBO							
	MAC LOVE							
	CHIC							
	COURT MASTERPIECE							

Although I was very excited about this landmark for the development of All-Weather racing in this country, I was also acutely aware that this contest was going to set quite a poser for me from a punting point of view. For one thing, half the field were trying sand for the first time, which is perhaps not surprising when you realise that an opportunity like this had never existed before. There were proven Group horses in the line up such as Chic and Autumn Glory, but how would they cope with Polytrack under race conditions? The fact is that no-one really knew.

The vibes about Chic had been very negative in the lead up to the race, so she looked a very shaky favourite, and I was still not convinced that Eccentric would be able to show his best if there was a frantic battle for the early lead. In this sort of situation, if I am going to have a bet, I will go with proven ability on the surface every time and as Vortex had also proven himself at Group Three level when beating Court Masterpiece on turf two week earlier, he had to be the one at the available odds, so I gladly took £320-£40.

The race went almost to plan. Vortex was nicely switched off at the back in a race run at a strong pace, and I was very hopeful when he arrived with what looked a race-winning challenge on the outside turning for home. Unfortunately, he could never quite maintain the effort and tired noticeably in the final furlong, only just managing to hold on for third behind Autumn Glory and Court Masterpiece. At least the winner was an established Group Three performer, so even though I hadn't won, the race had lived up to its status which was very good news.

The next contest on the card, a six-furlong nursery, looked a good opportunity to start clawing back some of that folding stuff.

2-30 LADBROKESGAMES.COM NURSERY (5) 2YO								
6 furlongs			Par = 94			11 runners		
AW FORM	NAME	BEST	LAST SIX					
21	CAMPBELTOWN	97W06					96L05	97W06
215	PICCOSTAR	95L05				90L05	85L05	95L05
1	LINDUS ATENOR	88W06						88W06
94	MUJELLE	84W06					77L05	84W06
3	BATHWICK ALICE	81L05						81L05
44	CASABLANCA MINX	79L05					78L05	79L05
	BELLA BERTOLINI							
	CAAN							
	MIDDLETON MINX							
	FRANKY'N'JONNY							
	FIGARO FLYER							

I really liked Campbeltown. Both his previous speed figures were higher than anything else in the field and he was proven on the surface and over the trip. He also had the assistance of Eddie Ahern and even though he was giving away upwards of 9lb to his ten rivals, it doesn't really matter when you have so many other factors in your favour. The only negative I could find was that he was starting from stall ten in an 11-horse field, but I still considered 4/1 so be a decent price and happily took £160-£40.

Even though the draw had seemed a negative, it was worth taking a chance that Eddie Ahern would be able to angle the colt across from his wide stall at some stage and then his class would surely see him through. Nice theory, but not as things turned out. Instead I found myself watching in total horror as Campbeltown was forced several horses wide on the first bend and then, after being unable to tuck in at any stage racing down the false straight, endured the same misfortune on the home turn as well! Considering the extra distance he must have travelled as a result, he did marvellously well to go down by just three-quarters of a length to Lindus Atenor. I felt robbed. This was definitely one that got away.

I didn't like the novice stakes that followed on the card, so had a coffee whilst the race was in progress and kept my powder dry for the one-mile handicap.

AW FORM	NAME	BEST	LAST SIX					
	3-35 LADBROKESCASINO.COM HANDICAP (0-80) (4) 3YO							
	8 furlongs		Par = 102		11 runners			
6212	RESPLENDENT NOVA	106W08			86L07	98L08	97L07	106W08
431-1	SWIFT OSCAR	106L08			91W06	92W07	96W08	106L08
00811	CASEMATE	102W07		66L08	85L08	86L08	97L08	102W07
44-	MR AITCH	98W09					93L08	98W09
76-	INNPURSUIT	91L10					90W08	91L10
3-	LORD OF DREAMS	89L08						89L08
	RED AFFLECK							
	WAVERTREE WARRIOR							
	PERUVIAN PRINCE							
	KEY OF SOLOMON							
	CURTAIN BLUFF							

Two horses dominated this race as far as I was concerned, Resplendent Nova and Swift Oscar. Both looked progressive and had earned speed figures well in excess of that required to win a race like this in their last outings on sand. I plumped for Swift Oscar, mainly because his big effort had come under identical conditions to these, so I felt that the £240-£40 I was able to get was quite fair.

Never have I been so confident during a race. Swift Oscar was always going like a dream and turning for home Richard Hughes was still travelling with a double-handful. When he hit the front a furlong out, I was congratulating myself on a job well done, but fate can quickly punish you for having such thoughts. So it was with complete horror that I watched Swift Oscar appear to pull himself up in front, hang over to the inside rail, and get caught on the line by Wavertree Warrior. I was beginning to think that this was not going to be my day.

The last race on a competitive card was a very tricky six-furlong handicap.

AW FORM	NAME	BEST	LAST SIX					
	4-05 LADBROKES HANDICAP (0-70) (5) 3YO+							
	6 furlongs		Par = 103		12 runners			
4194570-	HARD TO CATCH	107L06	101L06	101L06	101L06	102L07	96L07	80L07
17252371	OLD BAILEY	105S06	102S06	96S06	101S07	94S06	90W06	103S06
05915-05	EFFECTIVE	104L06	98S07	92L07	104L06	91W06	83W07	99L07
24052017	ADANTINO	103L07	89L07	95W07	02L06	92L06	101W06	97W06
54214606	RIQUEWIHR	102L06	99W07	102L07	92L07	90L07	95L06	102L06
/4973-00	POLAR FORCE	102L06	97L06	94L06	100L06	102L06	86S05	94L07
-1201435	MINIMUM BID	102L06	95L07	95L07	102L06	96L07	101L06	95L07
1/1	REZZAGO	101W06					95W07	101W06
65314-	SIMPSONS MOUNT	101L06		84L05	87L06	97L05	101L06	97L06
6/3-	DARLA	99L06					87L05	99L06
356-1415	MAJESTICAL	94L05	79W05	85W05	91W05	89S05	94L05	89W05
9/	GO GO GIRL	92L06						92L06

I found this race to be an absolute minefield and came up with a shortlist of three. Minimum Bid was racing over her best trip, Riquewihr had run better than it may have seemed on her last visit here and had shown her well-being with a recent win on turf, whilst the race looked sure to be run to suit Adantino and I could just see him coming fast and late to snatch the race on the line. Perhaps in hindsight I should have swerved the contest altogether, but the odds available on my three selections were high enough that if I backed them all and any of them won, I would be looking at quite a nice profit. I managed to get £480-£40 about Minimum Bid, £320-£40 about Riquewihr and £560-£40 about Adantino.

Unfortunately things didn't work out as I had hoped. In fact in this contest nothing was able to get into the race from off the pace and the four principals, including the winner Rezzago, were always to the fore. Minimum Bid did best of those held up in eventually finishing fifth, Riquewihr finished eighth whilst Adantino was always out the back and finished last.

I had held out such great hopes for this landmark meeting and whilst the occasion lived up to its billing as far as the Group race was concerned, the day had blown a big hole in the overall balance for the diary, which was unfortunate. I suppose I should have been happy that the total was healthy enough before the meeting started to absorb the fallout of a day like this and it would have been very easy to bemoan my luck with regards to both Campbeltown and Swift Oscar, but I won't do that because there are many other occasions when things do go my way. I just had to believe that with one more meeting scheduled for this diary, things were going to finish on a high.

Monday 9 August – Wolverhampton

The final meeting to be covered in this diary and I was determined to end it on an upward curve, but that's not to say I was going to treat the fixture any different simply because it was the last meeting. The methods used to formulate selections would be the same as always and the £40 level stake would also remain.

I wasn't going to get anything out of the first contest on the card, as things turned out. Two-year-old maidens on sand at this time of year aren't always no-bet races, as quite often one or two horses will already have shown decent form on the surface and have achieved a speed figure that would be enough to win a contest like this. That was true of this particular race, as a colt called Cavewarrior had run a figure close to the race par in his last outing and with improvement likely, he was probably going to be good enough.

The problem was that everyone else knew it too. He was tipped just about everywhere and opened up in the market at a shade of odds-on. I was hoping he might just drift to odds-against, especially when the money came for the second favourite Grecianette, but the other 11 runners were all very weak. As a result Cavewarrior's price also shortened and he went off at 8/11, so this became a no-bet race for me. He looked like a good thing to all and sundry, and ultimately he won like it.

The second race on the card was a 12-furlong conditions seller. A poor race, but plenty of sand form to go on and a contest I could really get my teeth into.

3-00 HOLIDAY INN DUNSTALL PARK SELLING STAKES (6) 3YO+								
12.2 furlongs			Par = 101	12 runners				
AW FORM	NAME	BEST	LAST SIX					
4/7-5521	DISTANT COUSIN	107L13	96S14	82L12	85S12	102W13	98L12	99L12
0208720-	INTERNATIONAL GUEST	107L10	94L12	74L12	95L08	97L12	107L10	91L10
-5222153	REGENCY RED	104S11	102W12	101W13	104S11	88W12	100W09	103W12
22-21	TRESOR SECRET	104L10			95L12	104L10	100W12	102W12
517-2437	YORK CLIFF	103W08	103W08	99W09	101W08	103W08	101W12	93W12
5120/0-	TWENTYTWOSILVER	102W07		85L07	93L07	102W07	95L07	89L10
-0252552	EZZ ELKHEIL	101L12	88W12	94W12	97W12	101L12	97W12	95L12
90-	XAARA DOON	85L08					77L07	85L08
	MISS TIDDLYPUSH							
	BEBE FACTUAL							
	SECOND PICK							
	HIGH FREQUENCY							

Distant Cousin appeared to be a strong contender and the only thing that counted against him in my mind was the absence of any worthwhile form on the Wolverhampton Polytrack. Admittedly his speed figure of 102 for finishing fifth of seven in a decent claimer here back in June was a fair effort, especially in the context of today's race, but he was beaten almost 17 lengths in that and there were a couple of others in this contest I was much more interested in.

The first one was Tresor Secret, whose record of one win and three seconds from four starts on sand marked him as a consistent sort and that counts for plenty in selling company. His speed figures were good, including on this surface, and being less exposed on sand than most of the other major players, there was a good chance he was capable of a bit more. Starting from stall one was no bad thing either, as the draw statistics in Chapter Four show. Suffice to say I really liked him and invested £40 at 100/30 with a deal of enthusiasm.

That wasn't my only investment in the race though. I saw Regency Red as another strong contender because of his string of consistent efforts over this course and distance since the new surface was laid, so I did something I hadn't done before during the course of this diary, I backed him each-way.

Quite why I did this is a bit hard to explain with no previous examples to draw on, but basically having gone through the race in detail I just couldn't find three horses that were better than him. Each-way betting isn't usually my cup of tea and I use the bet very sparingly, usually on something which is a monster price, so that if the horse in question runs the big race I expect him to without quite winning, at least I will get something out of him. The horse usually has to be a big price and Regency Red wasn't that, but he was available at 13/2 and as I was certain he would reach a place, backing him each-way meant that I was getting a free win bet on him with a small profit to come if he did make the frame.

The race eventually worked out perfectly, though it didn't look like doing so for a long time. Distant Cousin was sent into a clear lead soon after turning for home and didn't appear likely to be caught, but fortunately Tresor Secret found a fair turn of foot for a plater and came with a sustained run to get up and win by a neck. Regency Red confirmed my view of him as an each-way steal by finishing third.

The third race on the card was a seven-furlong nursery and again there was an odds-on favourite in Sir Mark Prescott's Outlook. I thought he would win, but was never going to get involved at odds of around 4/5. It's a good job he didn't drift to an attractive price though, as he got totally stuffed!

No such problems with the next race though, a tasty seven-furlong handicap and again plenty of sand form to go on.

4-00 BETFREDCASINO.COM HANDICAP (0-75) (5) 3YO+								
7.1 furlongs			Par = 103	12 runners				
AW FORM	NAME	BEST	LAST SIX					
40361150	BLUE EMPIRE	106W08	99W07	97W07	100W08	94W07	98W08	92L07
1/7-4	BORDER MUSIC	106L08				97L08	99L07	106L08
58048124	SILENT STORM	104W07	57S06	99L08	99W07	102L08	104W07	101W08
76750522	QUINCANNON	104S07	96W08	92W07	91W08	94W07	98W07	97W07
0-727644	YORKER	104S07	94W09	95W07	86W08	87W08	97W08	97W08
008114	CASEMATE	102W07	66L08	85L08	86L08	97L08	102W07	100L08
63-213	KAREEB	102W07		102L08	101L07	96L07	102W07	95L08
26-9	TRUMAN	101W08				101W08	93L10	90W08
960-0783	PARKVIEW LOVE	100W12	100W12	94W09	94W12	94S12	99L10	99W07
7-2	OUT OF INDIA	100W07					96W08	100W07
7-70	STATE DILEMMA	97L08				97W07	97L08	91W08
28	OWED	95W06					95W06	91W06

I like races like this, when everything looks so straightforward. The market leader was Casemate, but my speed figures showed that he hadn't quite reached the standard required to win an event like this, whereas Border Music and Silent Storm had done so relatively recently, and both were available at bigger prices!

Border Music was especially attractive. His fourth place in a hot handicap at Lingfield back in April showed that he was getting the hang of Polytrack and he had the scope to improve further on the surface, yet because of some ordinary efforts on turf in the meantime, his mark had dropped sufficiently so that today's race was the lowest grade he had ever found himself in. The booking of Jamie Spencer suggested stable confidence, he was well drawn in stall one (the 20/1 winner of the previous race over the same trip had also come from stall one) so once again I took £160-£40 in the belief that the result was going to be a positive one.

Just in case Border Music didn't fire for some reason, I also took £160-£40 about Silent Storm, as his recent form at this track entitled him to run a big race.

I was wrong about that though, because Silent Storm ran a modest race for no apparent reason, eventually finishing fifth, but to be honest the whole field was made to look very ordinary by Border Music. He was one of the easiest winners I had seen on sand for a long time, leading on the bit soon after turning in before striding away to win easing down by nine lengths.

By this stage I was hoping that the afternoon would carry on in the same vein, and that if it did I could break back through the £1000 profit barrier for the diary.

The next race gave me every confidence that I could achieve it here.

Staying events on sand have tended to be good to me over the years, as not that many horses truly see out the trip on the slower surfaces provided the pace is sound. It's particularly true at Southwell, but Wolverhampton is demanding enough to have made this race seem a decent opportunity.

4-30 WOLVERHAMPTON-RACECOURSE.CO.UK HANDICAP (0-55) (6) 4YO+								
16.5 furlongs		**Par = 101**	**13 runners**					
AW FORM	NAME	BEST	LAST SIX					
94-122	FRONTLINE FINANCIER	105W13		91S12	92W13	101W13	105W13	98L13
89271150	ANOTHER CON	102W12	100L10	96L10	99W09	100W12	89L12	83S12
33532-24	FIELD SPARK	102W12	97L12	87W12	95W16	86W12	102W12	99W13
14-13894	REFLEX BLUE	99W16	92S16	71W16	93W16	93W16	87W16	95W12
7-9016	OCEAN ROCK	98W13		83L12	86L10	80L13	98W13	98W13
20-91482	INDIAN CHASE	97W16	97L16	95W16	92S16	97W13	97W13	97W16
63	ARISTI	97W16					91W12	97W16
3167	DOUBLE ROYAL	97W13			95W12	94W12	97W13	94W13
2-59	CHESTALL	96S11				96S11	89S11	86W16
0	MISTER QUICKSAND	87L10						87L10
0/	GAELIC ROULETTE	85L12						85L12
60/	ETCHING	83L08					83L08	77W08
8/	AUTUMN FANTASY	82W16						82W16

Frontlinefinancier stood out a mile. He had good form at this track, and even though he hadn't won over this trip on sand before, he had won twice over it on turf earlier in the summer. Remember I said earlier that in most cases turf form should only be used as an indicator of an animal's well-being, rather than the true value of the form itself, and this was such a scenario. Frontlinefinancier's turf wins had suggested this trip was going to be within his compass, and that's all.

On the other hand, talking of indicators, his one outing since those two turf victories had given me a bit of cause for concern. He ran in the Goodwood Stakes at the Glorious meeting and admittedly faced a massive task in taking on decent rivals over two miles and five furlongs in heavy ground, and running from 8lb out of the handicap. Having said that, it would have been more reassuring had he performed a bit better than finishing a tailed-off last of the 14 runners. Was he going to still be feeling the effects of that effort today? That was a question no-one was going to know the answer to until he actually raced, but one thing I was sure of was that had he not run at Goodwood, I would have felt the same confidence about him today as I had done with Tresor Secret and Border Music earlier in the afternoon.

With the doubt about Frontlinefinancier, I had to find an alternative investment just in case he failed to sparkle and winkled out Field Spark, who had shown enough in similar contests at this track to suggest he would be there or thereabouts, though his stamina wasn't totally guaranteed. So I had £40 on Frontlinefinancier at 100/30 and took £160-£40 about Field Spark.

The other imponderable about this race, apart from Frontlinefinancier's well-being, was whether they would go a decent enough pace to suit him. Long-distance races at Wolverhampton are not run quite as slowly as they often are at Lingfield, but some are still not run at a true gallop and this was going to be such a race. I just wish Frontlinefinancier's jockey had been a bit more aggressive on a horse that was very likely to stay, yet would probably be caught out if the race turned into a sprint.

Needless to say, the race did indeed become a sprint over the last half-mile or so, and that didn't help Frontlinefinancier's cause at all. He came off the bridle in the back straight before plodding on to finish just over three lengths third behind the winner Aristi. Just how much his demanding Goodwood effort had taken out of him is impossible to say, because his performance didn't offer evidence either one way or the other, and the way the race was run gave him a feasible excuse in any case.

Field Spark ran a lifeless race back in sixth and rather suggested once again that he didn't stay, even in a race run at a moderate early tempo.

So to the last race in this diary, and a difficult one too, an apprentice handicap over the extended nine furlongs.

5-00 HOTEL AND CONFERENCING AT DUNSTALL PARK APPRENTICE HANDICAP (0-55) (6) 3YO+							
9.5 furlongs				Par = 101		13 runners	
AW FORM	NAME	BEST	LAST SIX				
5541174-	BRAVELY DOES IT	104W12	94W16	91W13	96W12	104W12	100W12	101W12
05232232	TROPICAL SON	102L10	101L10	96W09	99L10	98L13	100W13	95L12
0/4-6312	WE'LL MEET AGAIN	101W08	0S12	92S08	93S08	99W08	90W08	101W08
8842	DANCE IN STYLE	100S08			89W08	88W09	91W08	100S08
76255054	SPY GUN	100S06	100S06	86W07	92S06	84S07	87W08	98W08
/08-3723	BABY BARRY	99W08	81S08	81W08	96W07	86W08	99W08	90S08
4-34	MR BELVEDERE	97W12				96L10	97W12	91L12
06-791	TETCOTT	97W08		94L10	97W08	80S08	82W08	96W08
00460	BARRISSIMO	96W09		81S08	86L08	96L08	96W09	91W12
44632-79	HEATHYARDS JOY	93L08	80S08	83W06	90L07	93L08	75W07	86L06
6-480	BLAKE HALL LAD	92L08			92L08	86W09	0S07	70W12
7-0	ALPHA ECHO	80S06					80W09	80S06
	UNBRIDLED'S DREAM							

I got this race completely wrong from the very start. I was rather blinded by Bravely Does It's recent speed figures, even though they were achieved at the end of 2004. He had been running moderately on turf this year, but as we have seen before that wasn't necessarily a problem. This was more a 'Zimiri' situation than a 'Frontlinefinancier', but I should perhaps have paid more attention to the fact that all his best figures had come over much longer trips.

I also liked We'll Meet Again, as his previous form at the track was solid and the only niggling doubt was whether this trip was right on the limit of his stamina. I should have looked a bit closer at Dance In Style, but rather ignored her because she had seemed to improve when switched to Fibresand for the first time. I should have noticed that she was improving with racing in general, and that this longer trip on a faster surface than at Southwell was going to suit her, but I didn't do so and instead took £280-£40 about We'll Meet Again and £320-£40 about Bravely Does It.

I was right to be concerned about We'll Meet Again's stamina, as after pulling hard early in a prominent position, he faded to finish fourth behind the winner Dance In Style. Bravely Does It ran a stinker and finished a tailed-off last, which was much too bad for the shorter trip to have been the only reason.

So the meeting rather fizzled out after starting off so well and I had to content myself with the fact that at least I had made a profit on the day.

Diary Summary

An overall profit of £775 is fair enough from an opening balance of zero, but as is always the case with projects like this, you always feel that more money could have been made. Retrospective analysis is still a useful tool though, as it should eventually help weed out any recurring errors.

The profit for this diary is £55 more than that achieved in the first book, albeit from two fewer meetings and with a fixed £40 stake rather than variable stakes back in 2000. Of course, making a £1000 profit when Master Robbie scored at Lingfield back in March boosted the overall standing enormously and without him the running total would look very different.

This whole diary might suggest that the margin between success and failure is very narrow, a bit too close to Russian Roulette, and therefore too risky for many people with any pretensions to making betting on horses a greater part of their life, and possibly their income.

In response I would make this point. Take a look at how similar the situation was with Master Robbie going into the Lingfield contest with that of the Zimiri saga outlined in Chapter Five. Both horses had a record of one run, one win under identical conditions to those they were about to encounter. Their speed figures were competitive and by stripping away their turf performances they both became horses to be very interested in. Treating them that way made them wonderful value betting opportunities at 25/1 and 33/1 respectively, whether they won or not.

What I'm saying is that by using all or some of the methods outlined in this book, the likes of Zimiri and Master Robbie should be unearthed regularly enough to help return a profit in the long run. After all, it's not a question of how a profit is returned in the longer term, provided a profit is returned.

DETAILED SUMMARY OF BETS

Date	Track	Horse	Stake	Result	Profit/Loss	Balance
12/3	Wolv	Hiamovi	£40	2nd	–40.00	–40.00
		Katiypour	£40	Won 4/1	+160.00	+120.00
		Quiet Times	£40	Unp	–40.00	+80.00
		Garden Society	£40	2nd	–40.00	+40.00
		Night Air	£40	Won 3/1	+120.00	+160.00
		Don Pasquale	£40	3rd	–40.00	+120.00
		Moayed	£40	2nd	–40.00	+80.00
		Wessex	£40	2nd	–40.00	+40.00
		What-A-Dancer	£40	Unp	–40.00	0.00
19/3	Ling	Treasure Cay	£40	Unp	–40.00	–40.00
		Party Boss	£40	Won 9/2	+180.00	+140.00
		Mogaamer	£40	4th	–40.00	+100.00
		Corriolanus	£40	Unp	–40.00	+60.00
		Grand Passion	£40	Unp	–40.00	+20.00
		Master Robbie	£40	Won 25/1	+1000.00	+1020.00
		Lygeton Lad	£40	2nd	–40.00	+980.00
		Rydal	£40	3rd	–40.00	+940.00
		Katiypour	£40	4th	–40.00	+900.00
		Dance On The Top	£40	Unp	–40.00	+860.00
		Steely Dan	£40	Unp	–40.00	+820.00
2/4	Wolv	Dvinsky	£40	Unp	–40.00	+780.00
		King Nicholas	£40	Unp	–40.00	+740.00
		Bijou Dan	£40	2nd	–40.00	+700.00
9/4	Ling	Piccostar	£40	Won 9/4	+90.00	+790.00
		Diamond Max	£40	Unp	–40.00	+750.00
		Lygeton Lad	£40	Unp	–40.00	+710.00
		Moon Bird	£40	Won 5/1	+200.00	+910.00
		Girlsweekend	£40	3rd	–40.00	+870.00
		Rowan Pursuit	£40	2nd	–40.00	+830.00
28/5	Wolv	Farnborough	£40	2nd	–40.00	+790.00
		King At Last	£40	Unp	–40.00	+750.00
		Ferrara Flame	£40	4th	–40.00	+710.00
		Brenda Meova	£40	Won 8/1	+320.00	+1030.00
		Louisiade	£40	3rd	–40.00	+990.00
		Spark Up	£40	4th	-40.00	+950.00
9/7	Ling	Dancing Mystery	£40	Unp	–40.00	+910.00
		Odiham	£40	4th	–40.00	+870.00
		Vortex	£40	3rd	–40.00	+830.00
		Campbeltown	£40	2nd	–40.00	+790.00
		Swift Oscar	£40	2nd	–40.00	+750.00
		Minimum bid	£40	Unp	–40.00	+710.00
		Riquewihr	£40	Unp	–40.00	+670.00
		Adantino	£40	Unp	–40.00	+630.00
8/8	Wolv	Tresor Secret	£40	Won 10/3	+173.33	+803.33
		Regency Red	£40	EW3rd	+12.00	+815.33
		Border Music	£40	Won 4/1	+160.00	+975.33
		Silent Storm	£40	Unp	–40.00	+935.33
		Frontlinefinancier	£40	3rd	–40.00	+895.33
		Field Spark	£40	Unp	–40.00	+855.33
		We'll Meet Again	£40	4th	–40.00	+815.33
		Bravely Does It	£40	Unp	–40.00	+775.33

ROLL OF HONOUR
Horses with more than ten wins on sand before 31 July 2005

NAME	RUNS	WINS	2ND	3RD	UNP	% W/R
CHINA CASTLE	67	25	8	6	28	37.3
TEMPERING	89	22	13	9	45	24.7
RAMBO WALTZER	70	21	12	12	25	30.0
NO SUBMISSION	76	19	13	8	36	25.0
FAILED TO HIT	99	18	13	16	52	18.2
KINGCHIP BOY	79	17	6	3	53	21.5
ELTON LEDGER	78	16	20	5	37	20.5
KRYSTAL MAX	52	16	9	5	22	30.8
TAKHLID	56	16	6	6	28	28.6
ITALIAN SYMPHONY	59	15	8	9	27	25.4
NOUFARI	38	14	8	8	8	36.8
AFRICAN CHIMES	52	14	8	2	28	26.9
RAPPORTEUR	40	14	6	5	15	35.0
BANK ON HIM	55	13	14	8	20	23.6
WHITE PLAINS	75	13	12	13	37	17.3
FEAST OF ROMANCE	76	13	11	10	42	17.1
WESTERN COMMAND	132	13	10	14	95	9.8
BE WARNED	68	13	9	7	39	19.1
MALLIA	65	13	9	6	37	20.0
SWEET SUPPOSIN	55	13	6	9	27	23.6
JARAAB	26	13	3	1	9	50.0
PREMIER DANCE	89	12	14	16	47	13.5
MI ODDS	50	12	9	4	25	24.0
LAKOTA BRAVE	45	12	8	6	19	26.7
SIR TASKER	81	12	7	7	55	14.8
ON THE TRAIL	69	12	6	9	42	17.4
PALACEGATE TOUCH	70	11	13	10	36	15.7
ROYAL CASCADE	75	11	13	7	44	14.7
WEETMAN'S WEIGH	57	11	12	6	28	19.3
EVEZIO RUFO	92	11	10	15	56	12.0
BOLD ARISTOCRAT	94	11	9	17	57	11.7
RESPECTABLE JONES	53	11	9	9	24	20.8
SPENCER'S REVENGE	39	11	9	6	13	28.2
LITTLE IBNR	86	11	8	13	54	12.8
STATE APPROVAL	48	11	8	4	25	22.9
DAUNTED	49	11	7	10	21	22.4
ELITE HOPE	39	11	7	6	15	28.2
GREENSPAN	31	11	7	5	8	35.5
MASSEY	48	11	7	3	27	22.9
APOLLO RED	63	11	6	13	33	17.5
BLAKESET	25	11	5	2	7	44.0
SENSE OF PRIORITY	36	11	2	6	17	30.6
DESERT SPA	31	11	2	3	15	35.5

LINGFIELD					
Horses With Most Wins Per Track Before 31 July 2005					
NAME	**RUNS**	**WINS**	**2ND**	**3RD**	**UNP**	**% W/R**
RAPPORTEUR	40	14	6	5	15	35.0
KRYSTAL MAX	35	13	4	3	15	37.1
BANK ON HIM	47	12	11	7	17	25.5
RESPECTABLE JONES	48	11	9	9	19	22.9
APOLLO RED	59	11	6	13	29	18.6
AWESOME POWER	62	10	23	10	19	16.1
ONE OFF THE RAIL	30	9	7	5	9	30.0
LYGETON LAD	30	9	5	2	14	30.0
MASNUN	25	9	4	3	9	36.0
EL VOLADOR	18	9	3	2	4	50.0
INVOCATION	70	8	11	8	43	11.4
SPEEDY CLASSIC	43	8	9	8	18	18.6
ROBO MAGIC	43	8	8	4	23	18.6
SUPERCHIEF	60	8	7	7	38	13.3
NIGHT CITY	28	8	6	7	7	28.6
MR NEVERMIND	29	8	6	6	9	27.6
SWEET SUPPOSIN	36	8	5	8	15	22.2
DOUBLE M	45	8	5	6	26	17.8
LAKOTA BRAVE	25	8	5	4	8	32.0
STEELY DAN	33	8	5	3	17	24.2
AFRICAN CHIMES	27	8	4	1	14	29.6
SPENDER	27	8	3	5	11	29.6
URSA MAJOR	34	8	3	3	20	23.5
SIR TASKER	31	8	2	2	19	25.8
SARUM	79	7	13	11	48	8.9
BARBASON	45	7	7	11	20	15.6
WHITE PLAINS	32	7	6	4	15	21.9
BROUGHTONS FORMULA	30	7	5	4	14	23.3
STOPPES BROW	19	7	5	1	6	36.8
EASTLEIGH	39	7	5	1	26	17.9
PRINCE DANZIG	28	7	4	5	12	25.0
ECCENTRIC	15	7	4	0	4	46.7
ANOKATO	21	7	3	4	7	33.3
CASTLES BURNING	24	7	3	3	11	29.2
COLD TURKEY	17	7	3	2	5	41.2
PERSIAN CONQUEST	17	7	2	2	6	41.2
GOLDEN BRIEF	24	7	2	2	13	29.2
TAPAGE	14	7	1	1	5	50.0
NAUTICAL WARNING	22	7	1	1	13	31.8

SOUTHWELL
Horses With Most Wins Per Track Before 31 July 2005

NAME	RUNS	WINS	2ND	3RD	UNP	% W/R
TEMPERING	82	22	13	9	38	26.8
ELTON LEDGER	76	16	20	5	35	21.1
CHINA CASTLE	29	16	5	0	8	55.2
NO SUBMISSION	56	15	9	7	25	26.8
RAMBO WALTZER	36	13	10	4	9	36.1
KINGCHIP BOY	58	13	4	2	39	22.4
BOLD ARISTOCRAT	71	11	7	15	38	15.5
KYLKENNY	20	10	5	3	2	50.0
PICKENS	50	9	11	3	27	18.0
PINE RIDGE LAD	35	9	6	3	17	25.7
GAME GURU	30	9	2	5	14	30.0
MARENGO	81	8	9	6	58	9.9
WELLSY LAD	57	8	9	5	35	14.0
PHARLY DANCER	29	8	7	4	10	27.6
COUNT DE MONEY	18	8	4	4	2	44.4
KENT	22	8	4	1	9	36.4
BERGE	12	8	0	2	2	66.7
GREENSPAN	17	7	5	3	2	41.2
DAUNTED	21	7	4	3	7	33.3
MI ODDS	20	7	3	2	8	35.0
MASSEY	24	7	3	2	12	29.2
SENSE OF PRIORITY	20	7	1	4	8	35.0
HORIZON	11	7	0	0	4	63.6
STRAVSEA	54	6	10	7	31	11.1
DAHLIDYA	59	6	7	10	36	10.2
SEA DEVIL	21	6	7	3	5	28.6
SEA YA MAITE	67	6	6	12	43	9.0
WESTERN COMMAND	66	6	6	6	48	9.1
KEEN HANDS	43	6	6	1	30	14.0
TROJAN WOLF	37	6	5	5	21	16.2
KING PRIAM	51	6	5	4	36	11.8
MOONRAKING	22	6	5	3	8	27.3
BLAKESET	14	6	5	1	2	42.9
VINCENT	29	6	4	3	16	20.7
AFRICAN CHIMES	22	6	4	1	11	27.3
JOHNNIE THE JOKER	37	6	3	5	23	16.2
SUPER BENZ	22	6	3	4	9	27.3
JIBEREEN	28	6	3	3	16	21.4
BE WARNED	28	6	3	2	17	21.4
PENWELL HILL	16	6	3	1	6	37.5
VANBRUGH	15	6	3	0	6	40.0
COLONEL CUSTER	24	6	2	3	13	25.0
ROMIL STAR	14	6	2	1	5	42.9
CRECHE	20	6	2	1	11	30.0
QUIET TIMES	17	6	1	1	9	35.3
GOLDEN KLAIR	9	6	1	0	2	66.7
ORCHARD COURT	6	6	0	0	0	100.0

WOLVERHAMPTON
Horses With Most Wins Per Track Before 31 July 2005

NAME	RUNS	WINS	2ND	3RD	UNP	% W/R
FAILED TO HIT	65	14	9	13	29	21.5
NOUFARI	34	11	7	8	8	32.4
MALLIA	25	10	1	1	13	40.0
PREMIER DANCE	49	9	10	9	21	18.4
ELITE HOPE	30	9	7	5	9	30.0
TAKHLID	24	9	4	2	9	37.5
HILL FARM DANCER	48	9	3	10	26	18.8
FEAST OF ROMANCE	38	8	4	6	20	21.1
C-HARRY	42	8	4	6	24	19.0
RAMBO WALTZER	33	8	2	8	15	24.2
DESERT SPA	19	8	2	3	6	42.1
NIMELLO	14	8	0	1	5	57.1
FEATHERSTONE LANE	62	7	12	11	32	11.3
BRANSTON PICKLE	36	7	9	9	11	19.4
SUALTACH	41	7	7	5	22	17.1
ITALIAN SYMPHONY	30	7	5	5	13	23.3
BE WARNED	37	7	5	4	21	18.9
LITTLE IBNR	57	7	4	10	36	12.3
BARON DE PICHON	24	7	4	4	9	29.2
AROGANT PRINCE	33	7	4	2	20	21.2
STATE APPROVAL	21	7	4	1	9	33.3
WESTERN COMMAND	61	7	3	7	44	11.5
ON THE TRAIL	29	7	3	4	15	24.1
GILDED COVE	22	7	3	2	10	31.8
PRIDE OF BRIXTON	36	7	3	2	24	19.4
CHINA CASTLE	30	7	2	6	15	23.3
SOTONIAN	42	7	2	5	28	16.7
EVERSET	20	7	2	4	7	35.0
ROYAL CASCADE	51	6	9	4	32	11.8
WEET-A-MINUTE	21	6	6	1	8	28.6
EVEZIO RUFO	40	6	5	5	24	15.0
AREISH	20	6	5	3	6	30.0
MYSTERIUM	39	6	4	9	20	15.4
TIGRESS	27	6	4	5	12	22.2
WEETMAN'S WEIGH	30	6	4	1	19	20.0
BUSCADOR	16	6	3	0	7	37.5
WENTBRIDGE LAD	20	6	3	0	11	30.0
ARC EL CIEL	23	6	2	6	9	26.1
MISS GLORY BE	24	6	2	5	11	25.0
MIDSHIPMAN	12	6	1	1	4	50.0
INVER GOLD	17	6	1	1	9	35.3
SORBIESHARRY	29	6	0	5	18	20.7
FRENCH SPICE	8	6	0	0	2	75.0

HORSES WITH MOST FLAT WINS ON SAND
1989-2005

YEAR	NAME	RUNS	WINS	2ND	3RD	UNP	% W/R
1989*	THE SHANAHAN BAY	4	3	0	0	1	75.0
1990	{BRONZE CROSS	9	5	0	0	4	55.6
	{IRISH PASSAGE	10	5	0	2	3	50.0
	{RAPPORTEUR	11	5	1	3	2	45.5
1991	TEMPERING	12	5	1	1	5	41.7
1992	AFRICAN CHIMES	10	7	2	0	1	70.0
1993	TEMPERING	14	8	3	1	2	57.1
1994	EVERSET	13	7	1	3	2	53.8
1995	NO SUBMISSION	21	7	5	2	7	33.3
1996	{BERGE	7	5	1	1	0	71.4
	{PEOPLE DIRECT	15	5	2	3	5	33.3
1997	GLOBETROTTER	8	6	1	1	0	75.0
1998	ITALIAN SYMPHONY	24	9	6	6	3	37.5
1999	TAKHLID	18	11	2	1	4	61.1
2000	{FRENCH SPICE	7	6	0	0	1	85.7
	{SUPERCHIEF	16	6	3	1	6	37.5
2001	MADAME JONES	38	9	4	4	21	23.7
2002	{CHEENEY BASIN	15	7	4	0	4	46.7
	{LAKOTA BRAVE	15	7	2	3	3	46.7
2003	MI ODDS	14	6	4	0	4	42.9
2004	{FALL IN LINE	6	6	0	0	0	100.0
	{BROUGHTON KNOWS	14	6	2	1	5	42.9
2005**	{PARTY BOSS	5	5	0	0	0	100.0
	{FRATERNITY	8	5	1	0	2	62.5

* All-Weather Racing did not begin until October 30th

** Before July 31st

ORDER OF MERIT – HIGHEST ADONIS SPEED FIGURES
EARNED ON BRITISH ALL-WEATHER TRACKS
BEFORE 31 JULY 2005

Name	Date	Track	Dist	Gng	Typ	Pos	Ran	Weight	Drw	Pce	Rtng
REDBRIDGE	25APR1998	WOLV	12	SD	4M	1	6	9-12	2	P	122
NOUFARI	04JAN1995	WOLV	14.8	VF	4H	1	9	8-11	2	H	117
CRESKELD	01JAN2005	SOUT	8	SD	3H	1	12	8-7	3	L	117
WEET FOR ME	15DEC2000	SOUT	12	SD	3H	1	7	9-2	6	L	117
PINE RIDGE LAD	05FEB1996	SOUT	8	VS	4H	1	13	9-7	12	L	116
RAFFERTY	01JAN2005	SOUT	8	SD	3H	2	12	8-9	12	H	116
FALL IN LINE	26JAN2004	WOLV	12	SW	5H	1	12	9-0	4	L	116
HILLZAH	01DEC1993	SOUT	11	SD	5H	1	10	9-0	5	P	116
ECCENTRIC	19MAR2005	LING	10	SD	1N	1	14	8-12	1	L	116
OUR TOM	08JAN1996	SOUT	11	SD	4H	1	11	8-4	11	P	116
BAWSIAN	15DEC2000	SOUT	12	SD	3H	2	7	8-6	4	P	116
BOLD FRONTIER	08MAR1997	WOLV	5	SD	3H	1	9	7-12	5	H	116
CASTLE GANDOLFO	06APR2002	LING	8	SW	2N	1	10	8-11	9	H	116
IOTA	04JAN1995	WOLV	14.8	VF	4H	2	9	9-2	8	H	115
HIGH ACTION	09JUL2005	LING	16	SD	2H	1	13	9-2	7	H	115
JORROCKS	19JAN2001	SOUT	7	VS	3H	1	16	9-9	5	H	115

Name	Date	Track	Dist	Gng	Typ	Pos	Ran	Weight	Drw	Pce	Rtng
MRS JAWLEYFORD	14DEC1993	SOUT	16	SD	5H	1	14	7-12	2	P	115
HAIL THE CHIEF	26DEC2000	WOLV	9.4	SD	3H	1	13	9-9	2	L	115
CRETAN GIFT	28FEB1997	SOUT	6	SD	3H	1	12	9-9	12	H	115
BLYTHE KNIGHT	19MAR2005	LING	10	SD	1N	2	14	8-12	12	H	115
BELLA PAVLINA	16MAR2004	SOUT	12	SW	3H	1	9	7-6	7	P	115
CHIEF OF JUSTICE	15DEC2000	SOUT	12	SD	3H	3	7	7-7	5	P	115
FAR CRY	13MAR1999	WOLV	16.2	SD	4H	1	8	9-6	1	P	115
BALLYNAKELLY	06JAN1996	LING	12	SW	4H	1	10	7-13	9	P	115
DISKETTE	01DEC1993	SOUT	11	SD	5H	2	10	10-0	1	P	115
WEET FOR ME	08JAN2001	SOUT	11	SD	3H	1	15	9-9	11	L	115
RIVER KEEN	02DEC1995	WOLV	12	FT	3H	1	12	8-6	9	P	115
PUFF PUFF	10AUG1991	LING	16	SW	5H	1	8	8-12	6	H	115
SUPERSTRIKE	31JUL1991	SOUT	6	VS	6M	1	12	9-0	3	P	115
SIR FERBET	29NOV2000	WOLV	8.5	SD	3H	2	11	9-5	5	P	114
SHARMY	08FEB2003	LING	12	SD	2H	1	16	9-10	15	H	114
CHINA RED	07MAY1999	LING	8	SD	3H	1	7	8-11	2	L	114
CAESAREAN HUNTER	03SEP2003	LING	16	SW	5H	1	14	9-12	11	H	114
CORRIOLANUS	30NOV2004	LING	10	SD	3H	1	11	9-4	11	H	114
SUDEST	13MAR1999	WOLV	16.2	SD	4H	2	8	9-12	5	P	114
CHEWIT	09JAN1996	LING	6	SD	4H	1	13	10-0	9	H	114
AUTUMN GLORY	09JUL2005	LING	8	SD	G3	1	12	9-2	12	P	114
VORTEX	13MAR2004	WOLV	8.5	VS	2H	1	12	8-12	13	H	114
APPLEDORN	16JAN1993	LING	6	SW	5C	1	6	8-8	3	P	114
AIR MAIL	19JAN2001	SOUT	7	VS	3H	2	16	9-7	6	P	114
SWIFT SAILOR	09JUL2005	SOUT	16	SD	2H	3	13	9-3	11	H	114
CRECHE	05MAR1993	SOUT	6	VS	3H	1	7	9-8	6	L	114
UNCONDITIONAL LOVE	25NOV1997	LING	10	SD	4N	1	6	8-9	4	P	114
TE QUIERO	13MAR2004	WOLV	8.5	VS	2H	2	12	9-2	3	L	114
COURT MASTERPIECE	09JUL2005	LING	8	SD	G3	2	12	8-13	5	H	114
PRIMARY COLOURS	21NOV1998	WOLV	12	SD	2H	1	10	7-10	4	P	114
ONE DINAR	24FEB2000	WOLV	8.5	SD	3H	1	11	7-10	3	H	114
PERUVIAN CHIEF	23FEB2002	LING	5	SW	3H	1	10	9-7	3	P	114
HURRICANE ALAN	19MAR2005	LING	10	SD	1N	3	14	8-12	2	P	114
METEOR STRIKE	29DEC1998	LING	12	SD	3H	1	8	8-9	2	L	114
NIMELLO	10MAR2001	WOLV	8.5	SD	2H	1	12	10-0	9	H	114
NIGHT SIGHT	19MAR2001	SOUT	12	VF	3H	1	12	8-3	10	P	114
MILNGAVIE	14DEC1993	SOUT	16	SD	5H	2	14	7-11	11	P	114
HAIL THE CHIEF	29NOV2000	WOLV	8.5	SD	3H	1	11	8-11	2	L	114
RAMBO'S HALL	08JAN1996	SOUT	11	SD	4H	2	11	10-0	6	P	114
FLOWNAWAY	04DEC2002	SOUT	12	SD	6H	1	16	9-9	9	H	114
SUPER BENZ	15FEB1991	SOUT	6	VS	3H	1	7	9-5	2	L	114
DARGO	13MAR1999	WOLV	6.2	SD	4H	3	8	8-3	8	P	114
GOLDEN QUEST	09JUL2005	LING	16	SD	2H	2	13	8-11	5	P	114
PARASOL	15MAR2003	LING	10	SD	1N	1	14	9-10	5	L	114
POLAR KINGDOM	12FEB2004	SOUT	7	SD	3H	1	10	8-13	10	P	114
GENERAL	16MAR2004	SOUT	12	SW	3H	2	9	7-13	10	H	114